Study of Sorrow

Also by Shangyang Fang

Burying the Mountain

Study of Sorrow: Translations

Shangyang Fang

Copper Canyon Press
Port Townsend, Washington

Cover art: Ye Cheng, *Happy Excursion No. 7,* 2025.
Image courtesy of the artist and Latitude Gallery New York.
The Chinese calligraphic art featured in this book
is by Li Jiagang and Shen Zhiyu.

Copper Canyon Press is in residence at Fort Worden State Park
in Port Townsend, Washington, under the auspices of Centrum.
Centrum is a gathering place for artists and creative thinkers from
around the world, students of all ages and backgrounds, and
audiences seeking extraordinary cultural enrichment.

LIBRARY OF CONGRESS CATALOGING-IN-PUBLICATION DATA
Names: Fang, Shangyang translator
Title: Study of sorrow : translations / Shangyang Fang.
Description: Port Townsend, Washington : Copper Canyon Press, 2025. |
Includes index. | Summary: "A collection of poems translated by
Shangyang Fang"— Provided by publisher.
Identifiers: LCCN 2025021588 (print) | LCCN 2025021589 (ebook) |
ISBN 9781556597176 paperback | ISBN 9781619323193 epub
Subjects: LCSH: Chinese poetry—Translations into English | LCGFT: Poetry
Classification: LCC PL2658.E3 S75 2025 (print) | LCC PL2658.E3 (ebook) |
DDC 895.11008—dc23/eng/20250609
LC record available at https://lccn.loc.gov/2025021588
LC ebook record available at https://lccn.loc.gov/2025021589

9 8 7 6 5 4 3 2 FIRST PRINTING

COPPER CANYON PRESS
Post Office Box 271
Port Townsend, Washington 98368
www.coppercanyonpress.org

To my friends

Contents

离别 Departure

Study of Sorrow

Departure

木兰花・和孙公素别安陆

张先

相离徒有相逢梦。门外马蹄尘已动。
怨歌留待醉时听，远目不堪空际送。

今宵风月知谁共。声咽琵琶槽上凤。
人生无物比多情，江水不深山不重。

Departure

To the Tune "Mu Lan Hua: Magnolia"

Zhang Xian

After tonight, what's left of you is you
moving into my dream. Outside, the horse hooves
stamping the ground, the dust moves.
No sorrowful songs for me unless I am drunk.
I am drunk. Forgive me that I couldn't bear
to see you off, vanishing with the sun.
Alone with the west wind and the moon.
Alone listening to the pipa sobbing, its pegbox
carved into a phoenix. Listen, crying bird:
To live without this grief is to see the mountain
without its weight, rivers without depth.

点绛唇·丁未冬过吴松作

姜夔

燕雁无心，太湖西畔随云去。
数峰清苦。商略黄昏雨。

第四桥边，拟共天随住。
今何许？凭阑怀古。残柳参差舞。

Passing Song Wu in the Winter of 1187
To the Tune "Dian Jiang Chun: Rouged Lips"

Jiang Kui

Swallows and swans, heartless,
trail the rootless clouds at the west side of Lake Tai.

Thin hills stand still in bankruptcy,
discussing whether they could afford another rain

before sunset. I too wanted
to disappear with you at Fourth Bridge.

Friend, where are you now? Beyond
the railing, those broken willows dance so brokenly.

浪淘沙慢

周邦彦

晓阴重，霜凋岸草，雾隐城堞。南陌脂车待发，东门帐饮乍阕。
正拂面、垂杨堪揽结。掩红泪、玉手亲折。
念汉浦、离鸿去何许？经时信音绝。

情切，望中地远天阔。向露冷风清，无人处，耿耿寒漏咽。
嗟万事难忘，惟是轻别。翠尊未竭，凭断云、留取西楼残月。

罗带光消纹衾叠，连环解、旧香顿歇。
怨歌永、琼壶敲尽缺。恨春去、不与人期，弄夜色、空馀满地梨花雪。

To the Tune "Lang Tao Sha Man: Waves Sifting Sand Extended"

ZHOU BANGYAN

The sky leaden at daybreak, the riverbank grass frost-wilted, parapets
of the citadel consumed in fog. The axles of carriages all greased up
by the East Gate, where the farewell banquet draws to an end.
Tears medleyed with the rouge powder. You pick a thin sprig of willow,
soft and taut, and knot it into a bracelet. Beside the Han River,
swans passing overhead, and the sky is a letter not addressed to men.

Love hurts. These eyes are not designed to hold an earth and sky
so infinite. I walk to where streaks of wind sharpen the coldness of dew,
where the water clock drips all night, imitating human sadness.
Tell me, water clock, you who will not be injured by sorrow, how to get used
to these long, valedictory echoes. The jade cup isn't emptied.
By the West Tower, remnants of clouds holding over a damaged moon.

The silk-laced waistband has lost its luster. The quilt wrinkled like years.
The interlocked glass rings smashed. The scented sachet, just a sachet.
Singing sad songs to the night's end, beating time with a chopstick
on a crystal pot until one of them breaks. I hate that the spring always leaves
without forewarning—against the black of midnight,
a sheet of pear blossoms scattered on the ground, mistaken for first snow.

丑奴儿

秦观

夜来酒醒清无梦，愁倚阑干。
露滴轻寒，雨打芙蓉泪不干。

佳人别后音尘悄，瘦尽难拚。
明月无端，已过红楼十二间。

To the Tune "Chou Nü Er: Ugly Doll"

Qin Guan

I wake up lucid and dreamless, leaning
on the balcony. Autumn rain
falls on hibiscus. The night is weeping.

Since you left, I have grown thin.
The moon moves past twelve
red chambers without human noticing.

浣溪沙

晏殊

一向年光有限身，
等闲离别易销魂，
酒筵歌席莫辞频。

满目山河空念远，
落花风雨更伤春，
不如怜取眼前人。

To the Tune "Huan Xi Sha: Silk-Washing Brook"

Yan Shu

In time's light, I inhabit this finite body.
Out of nowhere, departures
emaciate the soul.
So stop declining banquets, wine, songs.

Rivers, limitless mountains fill the eyes
with empty distance.
Let alone people are flowerlike, windswept.
Look at me, as long as we breathe.

雨霖铃

柳永

寒蝉凄切，对长亭晚，骤雨初歇。
都门帐饮无绪，留恋处，兰舟催发。
执手相看泪眼，竟无语凝噎。
念去去，千里烟波，暮霭沉沉楚天阔。

多情自古伤离别，更那堪，冷落清秋节！
今宵酒醒何处？杨柳岸，晓风残月。
此去经年，应是良辰好景虚设。
便纵有千种风情，更与何人说？

To the Tune "Yu Lin Ling: Bells in Rain"

Liu Yong

The sound of cicadas pierces

the autumn sky; late against the pavilion,
the downpour stops

so suddenly. At the makeshift tent,
beyond the city gate of the capital, the wine,

tasteless. The docked boat
like a leaf of magnolia urges your leaving.

We hold hands, looking
so deeply into each other's eyes, tearful—

for the first time, I feel that more language
suggests more hopelessness.

Thinking of where
you are going—you are going

where masses of evening clouds envelop,
thicken over an infinite

stretch of mist-hooded waters.

✦

Those who laugh at me
for my sentimentality, come, step inside

this lover's shape
that cuts open this desolate autumn day.

To what will I wake
tonight? At the bank of poplars and willows,

where the dawn wind shears a slim moon.
There will still be years

ahead, good days that are embroideries
with enchanting images

continuing in emptiness. How they will invoke
a thousand feelings—a thousand

ravishments, agonies—
and I can't tell you about any of it.

唐多令・惜别

吴文英

何处合成愁。离人心上秋。纵芭蕉不雨也飕飕。
都道晚凉天气好，有明月、怕登楼。

年事梦中休。花空烟水流。燕辞归、客尚淹留。
垂柳不萦裙带住。漫长是、系行舟。

Departure

To the Tune "Tang Duo Ling: A Little Song"

Wu Wenying

What composes sorrow: autumn weighs on the heart:
          each departing lover: an autumn
on their heart: the plantain leaves mimic the pattering

of rain: without rain: the weather pleasant at evening:
          lambent moon: fear of ascending
the high pavilion: years recede in dreams: the emptiness

of the blossoms replaces all the blossoms: all is water
          behind the mist: composed of water:
swallows gone: the traveling guest remains: narrow

          branches of a willow tree: failed to tether
her silken sash: tethers unyieldingly my returning boat:

采桑子

吕本中

恨君不似江楼月，南北东西，南北东西，只有相随无别离。
恨君却似江楼月，暂满还亏，暂满还亏，待得团圆是几时？

To the Tune "Cai Sang Zi: Picking Mulberries"

Lü Benzhong

I hate that you are not like the moon over the river tower,
 sticking around at the south, the north,
the east and west. At the south, the north, the east and west,
 the moon doesn't abandon the river tower.

I hate that you are just like the moon, starting to wane
 the moment it waxed. The moment it wanes,
it begins to wax; the moon never completes itself. Without me,
 you complete yourself, residing in departure.

水调歌头

苏轼

明月几时有？把酒问青天。不知天上宫阙，今夕是何年。
我欲乘风归去，又恐琼楼玉宇，高处不胜寒。
起舞弄清影，何似在人间。

转朱阁，低绮户，照无眠。不应有恨，何事长向别时圆？
人有悲欢离合，月有阴晴圆缺，此事古难全。
但愿人长久，千里共婵娟。

To the Tune "Shui Diao Ge Tou: Song of Water"

Su Shi

Since when has the moon been up there?
Lifting my wine cup, I ask the sky. What season is it
for the immortals in the palace of clouds?
I would ride up there on the horses of gale, but I fear

the winter in the transparent palaces made
of crystal and onyx would erase my shadow. I dance
with my shadow and know it is still good
to be in this world. Curving past the crimson chamber,

the moon hangs low in the window to be with
the sleepless travelers. The moon shouldn't detest us mortals,
but why is it always beautiful when men part?
How we never get used to the joy in meetings, fear

parting, toyed with by the moon's wax and wane.
This brokenness we must get used to. Friend, I wish you
a long life from a thousand miles away.
Night after night, a moon hangs up in two windows.

鹧鸪天·代人赋

辛弃疾

晚日寒鸦一片愁。柳塘新绿却温柔。
若教眼底无离恨，不信人间有白头。

肠已断，泪难收。相思重上小红楼。
情知已被山遮断，频倚阑干不自由。

Written on Behalf of Someone
To the Tune "Zhe Gu Tian: Partridge Sky"

Xin Qiji

As usual, ducks dip in the pond,
the willow branches gilded
in the last warmth of sunset.
From the red tower, hills block away

the last of you. Had I not seen
so many departures in this
life, I wouldn't have believed
that in the end all hair grows white.

蝶恋花·早行

周邦彦

月皎惊乌栖不定，更漏将残，辘轳牵金井。
唤起两眸清炯炯。泪花落枕红绵冷。

执手霜风吹鬓影。去意徊徨，别语愁难听。
楼上阑干横斗柄，露寒人远鸡相应。

Aubade

To the Tune "Die Lian Hua: Butterflies Love Flowers"

Zhou Bangyan

Moon rises, startling a field of crows.
Timepiece depleted of liquid.
The golden well remains tethered to a rope.
Sound of winch turning
wakes up a pair of eyes brightened in tears
that smear red cotton quilt.

Dawn gust fingers back her tangled earlocks.
Words are inaudible, unnecessary.
Unbelievable constellations
revolve above our newly painted chamber.
In this region of icy dewdrops,
light footfalls echo a rooster's call.

贺新郎·别茂嘉十二弟

辛弃疾

绿树听鹈鴂。更那堪、鹧鸪声住，杜鹃声切。
啼到春归无寻处，苦恨芳菲都歇。算未抵、人间离别。
马上琵琶关塞黑，更长门、翠辇辞金阙。看燕燕，送归妾。

将军百战身名裂。向河梁、回头万里，故人长绝。
易水萧萧西风冷，满座衣冠似雪。正壮士、悲歌未彻。
啼鸟还知如许恨，料不啼清泪长啼血。谁共我，醉明月？

Sending Off My Cousin Mao Jia
To the Tune "He Xin Lang: Toasting the Bridegroom"

Xin Qiji

Those trees, paralyzed in their dark green, are forced to endure
the songbirds. When the partridges fade out,
the cuckoos pick up their affliction, keep strumming their thin
windpipes till the death of spring, death of all
flourishing, petals that are shattered porcelain, sharp to the sight—
all these are less unbearable than a man being
separated from another. Listen, you who are leaving me, tell me
again the legend of Wang Qiang in the Han dynasty:
When she was sent across the Ongi River, across that vast wasteland
of Mongolian plateau to marry the king of Xiongnu,
she played pipa on horseback—gut-ripping melody.
The migrating birds who overheard this desolation forgot
the knowledge of flight, flung themselves to the ground.
Consider Empress Chen deposed from her gold palace
on a jade palanquin to the grim Long Gate, how she spent her life
savings, ten thousand pieces of gold, pleading
with the poet to write the emperor the Ode of Long Gate in hope
of seeing him. Or consider the lines of the ancient poet
Zhuang Jiang on two swallows in the sky bound by an invisible thread,
witnessing the helpless separation of two lovers.

✦

Ruined was the general of Han, Li Ling, who after a hundred battles
chose to kneel in front of his enemies. Imagine
his friend, Su Wu, who upon release from his captivity in war,
after nineteen years in prison, had to bid farewell
to Li—how his heart must have been riven on that riverbank—imagine
how Su turned back for the last time; in that
final glance, a million miles were already placed between them.
Consider Jing Ke, before he was sent to assassinate
the king of Qin, by the cold bank of the Yi River; remember his song:
"The gale blows, the Yi River freezes. The hero
fords once, never to return." How Prince Dan and all the guests
wore white gowns and white hats for his departure—
the whole capital an empire of snow. The parting was already a funeral.
Had the wailing birds known of such deep
sorrow, their singing would have been rhymed with coughs of blood.
After tonight, who would come by to get drunk
with me, on flowers that are wine jars loaded with distilled moonlight?

Lovesickness

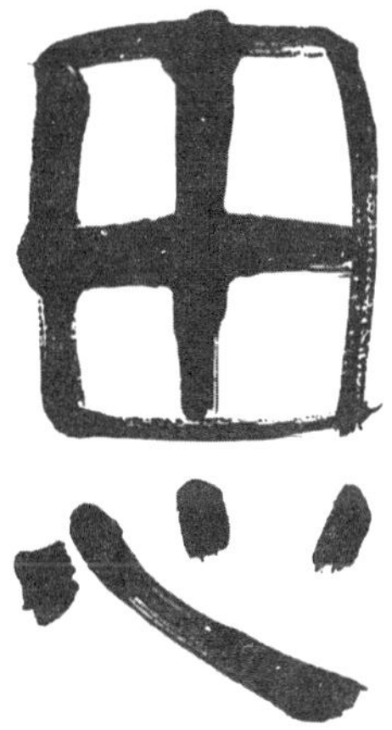

醉花阴

李清照

薄雾浓云愁永昼，瑞脑销金兽。
佳节又重阳，玉枕纱厨，半夜凉初透。

东篱把酒黄昏后，有暗香盈袖。
莫道不销魂，帘卷西风，人比黄花瘦。

To the Tune "Zui Hua Yin: Drunk in the Shadow of Flowers"

Li Qingzhao

These are long days. Days of waiting
stretched longer by the clouds

thickening over the weak fog,
and the smoke of burnt camphor

rising from the golden incense box.
Once again, it is the Chongyang Festival.

Jade pillow and gauze tent,
a coldness permeating the midnight.

Holding a cup of rice wine
at the East Fence; my sleeves filled

with the odor of old blossoms.
Don't tell me that the soul

won't be abraded by this dense scent
of lovesickness. The west wind

rolling up the curtain, I am thinner
than a yellow chrysanthemum.

夜游宫

吴文英

人去西楼雁杳。叙别梦、扬州一觉。
云澹星疏楚山晓。听啼乌，立河桥，话未了。

雨外蛩声早。细织就、霜丝多少。
说与萧娘未知道。向长安，对秋灯，几人老。

To the Tune "Ye You Gong: Night Tour at the Palace"

Wu Wenying

The west tower emptied of crowds:
          and clouds, of geese: reciting my dreams
to you in a dream after separation:
          one nap in Yangzhou that lasts a decade:
before words complete themselves:
          crows cry: collapsing the bridge
in sleep: faint stars above Chu Mountain
          obscured by fog and aurora:

Rain persists: crisscrossed with the wretched
          wails of crickets: cold: as if:
weaving the air into infinite shreds of frost:
          my heart I cannot tell you:
I cannot tell you the time: facing Changan City:
          facing the autumnal lamps:
Tell me: what is more rancid than death: dying: no:
          we must grow old without love:

暗香

姜夔

旧时月色，算几番照我，梅边吹笛？
唤起玉人，不管清寒与攀摘。
何逊而今渐老，都忘却春风词笔。
但怪得竹外疏花，香冷入瑶席。

江国，正寂寂，叹寄与路遥，夜雪初积。
翠尊易泣，红萼无言耿相忆。
长记曾携手处，千树压、西湖寒碧。
又片片、吹尽也，几时见得？

To the Tune "An Xiang: Dim Scent"

Jiang Kui

Aged moonlight, how many times

have you shone on me, beside the plum blossoms?
Listening to sounds of the flute.

Wake up, love—despite the air being cold
like washed jade, we climbed

to pluck the newest buds. Now,
as I've aged, my oblivious brushstrokes too weak

to recite the spring wind, the sparse,
rose-colored dapples beyond the bamboo forest

sending a sharp fragrance.

✦

The water provinces, desolate.

I want to send you this sprig of plum blossoms
tonight. Tonight, snow piles

for ten thousand miles. The emerald wineglass
weeps against the red calyx.

Remember where we held hands, the moment
when a hundred trees suddenly

bent crimson beside a lake.
Then piece by piece, taken by the wind.

These assembled pasts . . . when, again, will I see?

清平乐

赵令畤

春风依旧，著意隋堤柳。
搓得鹅儿黄欲就，天气清明时候。

去年紫陌青门，今宵雨魄云魂。
断送一生憔悴，只消几个黄昏？

To the Tune "Qing Ping Yue: Melody of Serenity"

Zhao Lingzhi

On the Sui Embankment, spring wind
hasn't changed a bit, kneading
willow sprouts till they turn light yellow,
the texture of duck feathers.
Last year, we walked on the purplish
pathway to the city gate.
Tonight, clouds after rain
assemble a loose apparition of you.
How many more sunsets
can a heart endure? Expectancy
thins me, and the twilight can kill a man.

风入松

吴文英

听风听雨过清明。愁草瘗花铭。
楼前绿暗分携路，一丝柳、一寸柔情。
料峭春寒中酒，交加晓梦啼莺。

西园日日扫林亭。依旧赏新晴。
黄蜂频扑秋千索，有当时、纤手香凝。
惆怅双鸳不到，幽阶一夜苔生。

To the Tune “Feng Ru Song: Wind Passing Through Pines”

Wu Wenying

Before Qingming Festival: days spent listening:
    to the rain, the wind that brought forth the rain:
sagging the grass: petals on earth: like etched words

on a tombstone: the barren path where we parted:
    now light green crushed upon dark green:
each inch of willow is an inch of softness:

I drink in the cold of early spring: early spring dream
    dissolves in the warblers’ call: daily
I sweep the pavilion and the terrace at the West Yard:

wasps push the swing rope: on which your slim hand
    dented a scented scar: untouched
by footsteps: overnight: stairs grown wildly with lichens:

青玉案

贺铸

凌波不过横塘路，但目送、芳尘去。
锦瑟华年谁与度？月台花榭，琐窗朱户，只有春知处。

碧云冉冉蘅皋暮，彩笔新题断肠句。
试问闲愁都几许？一川烟草，满城风絮，梅子黄时雨。

To the Tune "Qing Yu An: The Green Jade Bowl"

He Zhu

Your footsteps so light they could tread on water.
Your leaving shadow—silken-
stepped and scented—petals blown in a gust.

Youthful years—mellifluous
and plush like strings of a garnished harp—spent
without you, wasted.

The moon halts to gaze at flowers.
Is it true that only the spring breeze can find you?

Clouds cerulean before rain
skulk above the highland of wild ginger.

I pick up the brush-pen. I fail to put down a line.

If you ask me how heavy
this lovesickness is—a sweep of mist-sheathed grasses,
a city flushed with flying catkins,

or this sudden downpour
when sunset is yellowed by plums' yellowing.

鹧鸪天・元夕有所梦

姜夔

肥水东流无尽期。当初不合种相思。
梦中未比丹青见，暗里忽惊山鸟啼。

春未绿，鬓先丝。人间别久不成悲。
谁教岁岁红莲夜，两处沉吟各自知。

New Year's Eve
To the Tune "Zhe Gu Tian: Partridge Sky"

Jiang Kui

The Fei River runs eastward without end.
        Had we not planted love,
love would have spared us this ache.
        In dream, your face seems less
accurate, palpable than in the painting,
        which is lost. I am lost in cries
of crows wrecking my dream of you.
        Spring hasn't grown green yet.
My sideburns, two patches of snow.
        In this world, there is no grief
when breakup outlasts memory.
        Tonight, all lanterns are lit red
like large lotuses in summer days, an ache
        inside me with its source missing.
        You must have felt the same.

踏莎行·自沔东来丁未元日至金陵江上感梦而作

姜夔

燕燕轻盈，莺莺娇软。分明又向华胥见。
夜长争得薄情知，春初早被相思染。

别后书辞，别时针线。离魂暗逐郎行远。
淮南皓月冷千山，冥冥归去无人管。

Recording a Dream on Jinling River, New Year 1187
To the Tune "Ta Suo Xing: Treading on Purple Nutsedge"

Jiang Kui

Light-winged as a swallow touching another swallow,
soft-voiced as a warbler calling warblers;

I can't tell whether it's you or my memory speaking
to me again: you, who are clueless

about my long nights, causing this beginning of spring
saturated with love's sickness. Letters

you sent me. Your needlework remains deeply stitched
along the inner lining of my coat.

To make me dream of you, your little soul
must have crept outside your body to travel

near my hairpin. The moon of Huainan, burnished
in coldness, freezes a thousand mountains

in one night. When your soul walks back, she walks back
alone, abandoned like the rest of us.

鹧鸪天

吴文英

池上红衣伴倚阑，栖鸦常带夕阳还。
殷云度雨疏桐落，明月生凉宝扇闲。

乡梦窄，水天宽。小窗愁黛淡秋山。
吴鸿好为传归信，杨柳阊门屋数间。

To the Tune "Zhe Gu Tian: Partridge Sky"

Wu Wenying

Lakeside vermilion dresses: lotuses lean
languid beside the balustrade:
ravens return: purloining a shard of sunset

behind the satin darkness
of their wings: rain, too, darkening: shaving
off more sycamore leaves:

moon in autumn sky: the inaugural coldness
that sets the folding
silk fan neglected by its familiar hand:

dream of homeland: narrow: porcelain clouds
above the water: vast:
the squared mountains in the window frame:

fog-thinned: the pigment
of painted eyebrows: twitching: mute swans
from the land of Wu carrying

letters to the houses behind the poplar trees
outside the Chang Gate:

蝶恋花

晏殊

槛菊愁烟兰泣露，罗幕轻寒，燕子双飞去。
明月不谙离恨苦，斜光到晓穿朱户。

昨夜西风凋碧树，独上高楼，望尽天涯路。
欲寄彩笺兼尺素，山长水阔知何处？

To the Tune "Die Lian Hua: Butterflies Love Flowers"

Yan Shu

Haze above the sill
is the chrysanthemums' language
for sorrow. Orchids

shed dew. Chill seeps in.
In pairs, swallows
gone. The moon, failing

to puzzle out the pain
of partings, shines through
a red mansion till dawn.

Last night, west wind
shook emerald off the trees.
On the high tower,

I memorized each route
to earth's edge.
Arranging my mind to words—

broad waters, ridges
thousandfold, feelings dashing
restlessly to nowhere.

蝶恋花·春景

苏轼

花褪残红青杏小，燕子飞时，绿水人家绕。
枝上柳绵吹又少。天涯何处无芳草。

墙里秋千墙外道，墙外行人，墙里佳人笑。
笑渐不闻声渐悄。多情却被无情恼。

Springtime

To the Tune "Die Lian Hua: Butterflies Love Flowers"

Su Shi

When the blossoms' scarlet is laved pink,
apricots appear green and tiny.
Swallows flit above the creek,
crossing a village. Cottonwoods
have used up their fluff.
But somewhere in this world,
there's always flowering.
The boy in the alley hears a girl's laughter
on the other side of the bluestone wall.
He listens till the laughter vanishes.
One with a soft heart
is meant to be harmed by the heartless.

千秋岁

张先

数声鶗鴂，又报芳菲歇。
惜春更把残红折。
雨轻风色暴，梅子青时节。
永丰柳，无人尽日花飞雪。

莫把幺弦拨，怨极弦能说。
天不老，情难绝。
心似双丝网，中有千千结。
夜过也，东窗未白凝残月。

To the Tune "Qian Qiu Sui: A Thousand Autumns Old"

Zhang Xian

The plump cuckoo cries, foreshadowing the end
of all florescence. To keep the spring, I snip off
a sprig of sighing scarlet. The plums turn green
in the light rain. A willow in the deserted yard
pieces together a snow day with its flying fluffs.
Don't touch the sharp pipa strings that reveal
to us our own insufferable heartache. The heart
is a messy net laced with a thousand loops, ten
thousand knots. As long as the sky doesn't grow
old, love shall not see its end. Night has ended.
At my east window, the broken moonlight congeals.

玉楼春

周邦彦

桃溪不作从容住，秋藕绝来无续处。
当时相候赤阑桥，今日独寻黄叶路。

烟中列岫青无数，雁背夕阳红欲暮。
人如风后入江云，情似雨馀粘地絮。

To the Tune "Yu Lou Chun: Jade Tower in Spring"

Zhou Bangyan

One mustn't live in the mythic Peach Creek
and forget about reality.
We become the snapped segments of a lotus root

which remain connected by thin, tenuous threads—
can't be sewn back together.

Now as I return to the Crimson Bridge,
the beige leaves pile up.
The mountaintops, blackish and countless,
tear through the broad mist,

and the geese with their backs turned
against the sunset are towing away sky's last violet.

Life is a walk through the wind, into the haze
above the far waters,

while heaving a grief
light as the cottonwood fluff, weighed down in rain,
adhering to the dank dark earth

江城子·乙卯正月二十日夜记梦

苏轼

十年生死两茫茫，不思量，自难忘。
千里孤坟，无处话凄凉。
纵使相逢应不识，尘满面，鬓如霜。

夜来幽梦忽还乡，小轩窗，正梳妆。
相顾无言，惟有泪千行。
料得年年肠断处，明月夜，短松冈。

Dreaming of My Wife in the First Month of 1075

To the Tune "Jiang Cheng Zi: River City"

Su Shi

For ten years we are separated
by a papery mist, as the living and the dead.

Even if you have come back to life,
you must not recognize me—a dusty face,
hair turned to frost.

In a dream, you came back,
beside the pinewood chamber, combing
your thick, black hair.

We looked at each other with no words—
a thousand lines of tears.

Wind crossing the short pines
we planted on the knoll.
Moonlight. Sound of our hearts shriveling.

踏莎行

吴文英

润玉笼绡，檀樱倚扇。绣圈犹带脂香浅。
榴心空叠舞裙红，艾枝应压愁鬟乱。

午梦千山，窗阴一箭。香瘢新褪红丝腕。
隔江人在雨声中，晚风菰叶生秋怨。

To the Tune "Ta Suo Xing: Treading on Purple Nutsedge"

Wu Wenying

The jade's sleek skin leaks scrubbed light:
arm bare, chiffon
swathed: a quarter slice of cherry
shaken by its own reddening: lips
concealed behind a folding fan's
unfolding: silk scarf dim-scented
with rouge powder: skirt in dance
pleated by the wind's many hands:
tucked like the many hearts of one
pomegranate: a stalk of mugwort
quenches the black hair's disquiet—

Noon's porous dream that implores
the diminishment of the distance:
ten thousand bodies of water closing:
all happened: when the shade
of an orchid shifts from the right side of
the casement to the left: the wrist's
ligature mark slowly disappearing:
its bracelet remains: you stand on
the other side of the deluge past a veil
of loud rain: listen: the bulrushes
lean back toward their own coldness:
giving birth to a real autumn—

Wartime

扬州慢

姜夔

淮左名都，竹西佳处，解鞍少驻初程。
过春风十里。尽荠麦青青。
自胡马窥江去后，废池乔木，犹厌言兵。
渐黄昏，清角吹寒。都在空城。

杜郎俊赏，算而今、重到须惊。
纵豆蔻词工，青楼梦好，难赋深情。
二十四桥仍在，波心荡、冷月无声。
念桥边红药，年年知为谁生。

To the Tune "Yangzhou Man: Slow Tune of Yangzhou"

Jiang Kui

The former metropolis on the left bank of the Huai River . . .
At the west side of Bamboo Pavilion,
I take the saddle off my horse, ask for a cup of water.

The bustling downtown was known once
as Ten Miles of Spring Breeze
and is now filled with patches of wheat and rapeseed.

Since the barbarous horses of the barbarous armies
peeked at this river, the derelict lakes
and burnt trees remain terrified of discussing war fire.

The death of the sun is approaching. The bleak sound
of a bugle rises in the evening cold,
charging this ramshackle city with complete emptiness.

✦

Had the late Tang poet Du Mu come back to life
to visit this city he loved so deeply,
he would have been transfixed in terror.

Even after his deft lines about the cardamom girls,
his spring dream at the Palace of Deviant Sensuality,
he could not transcribe this devastation.

By chance, the Twenty-Four Bridges remain.
Underneath them, each wavelet is a heart, pulsing with no end,
and the reflection of moon, snowlike in soundlessness.

I care only for the peonies weeping red
beside the bridges; year after year, they grow restlessly,
year after year, opening themselves for whom?

秋波媚・七月十六日晚登高兴亭望长安南山

陆游

秋到边城角声哀，烽火照高台。
悲歌击筑，凭高酹酒，此兴悠哉！

多情谁似南山月，特地暮云开。
灞桥烟柳，曲江池馆，应待人来。

Gazing from Afar at the Capital on July 16
To the Tune "Qiu Bo Mei: Soft Glances"

Lu You

Autumn has reached the villages on the frontier.
The bugle whimpers. The beacon towers are lit.
Enemies are coming. The soldiers are strumming
the zhu zither, singing death songs. Wine is poured
in libation for the dead to keep the dead from
returning to us. The moon over the southern hills
pushes open the evening clouds. We turn back
to look at the willows enveloped in cooking smoke,
the known alleyways and pavilions beside the Qu River
in the capital. They've almost forgotten our faces.

满庭芳

秦观

山抹微云，天连衰草，画角声断谯门。
暂停征棹，聊共引离尊。多少蓬莱旧事，空回首、烟霭纷纷。
斜阳外，寒鸦数点，流水绕孤村。

销魂当此际，香囊暗解，罗带轻分。
谩赢得、青楼薄幸名存。此去何时见也？襟袖上、空惹啼痕。
伤情处，高城望断，灯火已黄昏。

To the Tune "Man Ting Fang: Courtyard Blossoms"

Qin Guan

Clouds wipe off a fraction of the mountain.
Sky's hem sewn to desiccated grass.

The blare of a bugle intermittent on the watchtower.
We anchor the boat,
pour rice wine into cups, recounting

our stories about love
in wartime, where the lovers' faces are overlaid
with the faces of the dead,
until the evening mist takes over our memories.

Where the sunset cannot reach,
a burnt village,
few blotches of ducks dipping in the icy brook.

✦

Dim-lit hour, any soul would snap in half.

I untie my scented pouch,
loosen my girdle. The satin robe hanging on the chair

is another wretched man percolated
with copious tears.

Will we ever meet again in this mortal world?
I climb to the top of the watchtower.

At the limit of the sky,
people light up their windows with bulrushes
and lanterns, an extension of twilight.

西河・金陵怀古

周邦彦

佳丽地。南朝盛事谁记。山围故国绕清江，髻鬟对起。
怒涛寂寞打孤城，风樯遥度天际。

断崖树，犹倒倚。莫愁艇子曾系。
空余旧迹郁苍苍，雾沉半垒。夜深月过女墙来，伤心东望淮水。

酒旗戏鼓甚处市。想依稀、王谢邻里。燕子不知何世。
入寻常巷陌人家，相对如说兴亡，斜阳里。

Nostalgia at Jinlin
To the Tune "Xi He: West River"

Zhou Bangyan

Who remembers the prosperity of the Southern dynasty?
River-bounded Jinlin city, and in the suburbs
mountains echoing an infinite green. Among the tall waves
of the Yangtze, the merchant boats weaving the horizon.

Who remembers those lavish ships tethered beside the Lake
of Forgotten Sorrow? Now all that's left are these old
trees clung to their uninhabitable cliffs. Dense fog
sinking half the city. The moon is a poet, climbing over

the occupied rampart to stare at the Qinhuai River all night.
Where are those streets of yesterday, filled with banners
and flowers and gongs and drums? Those swallows
that used to nest beneath the painted eaves at the mansions

of aristocratic families now fly into the households
of ordinary people. Not knowing what dynasty
it is now, they cluster at the mud puddle by a porch,
debating the rise and fall of an empire in the slanted sun.

柳梢青・春感

刘辰翁

铁马蒙毡，银花洒泪，春入愁城。
笛里番腔，街头戏鼓，不是歌声。

那堪独坐青灯。想故国、高台月明。
辇下风光，山中岁月，海上心情。

Feelings in Spring

To the Tune "Liu Shao Qing: Green Willow Sprouts"

Liu Chenweng

In this occupied district, soldiers in wool felts
ride ironclad horses
through burnt woods. Fireworks toss

silver sparks like tear streaks of the night sky.
Spring came regardless to this city
assembled with skeletons. Foreign melodies

come from local flutes, each drumbeat
followed by a shriek. Those are not songs.
The lamp flickers green. I sit thinking of the lost

capital: high terrace where the moon shines.
My people, where are you?
Years in the mountains. Hearts on the sea.

渔家傲·秋思

范仲淹

塞下秋来风景异，衡阳雁去无留意。
四面边声连角起，千嶂里，长烟落日孤城闭。

浊酒一杯家万里，燕然未勒归无计。
羌管悠悠霜满地，人不寐，将军白发征夫泪。

Thoughts in Autumn

To the Tune "Yu Jia Ao: Pride of Fishermen"

Fan Zhongyan

Deep autumn, the geese flocks migrating
to Hengyang won't stop here.

They are tired of the landscape at this frontier fortress
and the monotone of bugles,
horses and cattle calling from all directions.

Among the vast mountain chains,
a lone city at sunset
where narrow cooking smokes rise behind the bulwark.

After a pot of turbid wine, my heart travels home
across ten thousand miles. But the war
hasn't ended. The sad melody from the Qiang flute
freezes the air. Snow falls on tents.

No one sleeps. The soldiers stand
silent in tears, hair whiter than their frosted land.

永遇乐·京口北固亭怀古

辛弃疾

千古江山，英雄无觅，孙仲谋处。
舞榭歌台，风流总被，雨打风吹去。
斜阳草树，寻常巷陌，人道寄奴曾住。
想当年，金戈铁马，气吞万里如虎。

元嘉草草，封狼居胥，赢得仓皇北顾。
四十三年，望中犹记，烽火扬州路。
可堪回首，佛狸祠下，一片神鸦社鼓。
凭谁问：廉颇老矣，尚能饭否？

Nostalgia at Beigu Pavilion, Jingkou

To the Tune "Yong Yu Le: Everlasting Joy"

Xin Qiji

Among these rivers and mountains that have endured
quietly for ten thousand years, it's hard to find the heroism
once seen in Sun Quan of Three Kingdoms.
Those waterside pavilions and resplendent terraces

for romantic entertainment have long been washed away
by persistent storms. Or beside the groves
half touched by slanted sun, an ordinary alleyway,
where the emperor Liu Yu once grew up impoverished.

Lost days—with golden spears and iron horse hooves,
Liu recaptured ten thousand miles of land
in one breath, like a truculent tiger.
But in our time, the indiscreet emperor miscalculated tomorrows,

resulting in a northern expedition where soldiers' tears
formed yet another unending river. That
was forty-three years ago—broad avenues in Yangzhou,
wrapped in a sea of flames—and was like yesterday.

If you look back in history, under the Bili Shrine,
the people worshipped a foreign king who had slaughtered
their parents and ancestors, where a crowd
of crows tore human flesh in the barrage of sacrificial drums.

Whom should we dispatch back to a thousand years ago,
to inquire whether the great general Lian Po,
though aged and broken, still has his mighty appetite?
Dead general, can you still lift your ashen bow and arrows?

菩萨蛮·书江西造口壁

辛弃疾

郁孤台下清江水，中间多少行人泪。
西北望长安，可怜无数山。

青山遮不住，毕竟东流去。
江晚正愁余，山深闻鹧鸪。

At Zaokoubi Battlefield, Jiangxi

To the Tune "Pu Sa Man: The Bodhisattva's Headdress"

Xin Qiji

The river that crosses
    the Yugu Terrace flows
        lucent and quiet

How much of that
    is the migrants' tears
        mixed in there

I gaze into the distance
    the conquered capital
        at the northwest

I see only mountains
    too many mountains
        mountains that can't

hold the river back
    from rushing eastward
        Dusk falls on water

From the depth of hills
    a quail's cry
        drills into my chest

燕山亭·北行见杏花

赵佶

裁剪冰绡，轻叠数重，淡著胭脂匀注。
新样靓妆，艳溢香融，羞杀蕊珠宫女。
易得凋零，更多少、无情风雨。愁苦，问院落凄凉，几番春暮。

凭寄离恨重重，者双燕，何曾会人言语。
天遥地远，万水千山，知他故宫何处。
怎不思量，除梦里、有时曾去。无据，和梦也新来不做。

Seeing Apricot Blossoms in Exile to the North

To the Tune "Yan Shan Ting: Pavilion on Yan Hill"

Zhao Ji

Meticulously the ice silk is tailored,
swathed and imbricated in thin layers, dappled,
anointed with rouge powder,
so it is in fashion, and fragrant,
putting ladies in the Pearl Bud Palace to shame.
So, it is too beautiful to last,
favored by storms. Visitation of indifferent
weather—the courtyard, tired
and bitter, faces yet another decline of spring.

Here's my handkerchief of grief—
paired swallows, for me will you deliver this
coarse, human language,
but to whom?—old palaces of my known past,
burned, stomped to dust.
I could only return to them in dreams
sometimes, dreams without cause or sources—
O silly, rootless things—luckily,
even they haven't come to me in recent nights.

桂枝香·金陵怀古

王安石

登临送目，正故国晚秋，天气初肃。
千里澄江似练，翠峰如簇。归帆去棹残阳里，背西风，酒旗斜矗。
彩舟云淡，星河鹭起，画图难足。

念往昔，繁华竞逐，叹门外楼头，悲恨相续。
千古凭高对此，谩嗟荣辱。六朝旧事随流水，但寒烟衰草凝绿。
至今商女，时时犹唱，后庭遗曲。

Nostalgia at Jinlin

To the Tune "Gui Zhi Xiang: Fragrant Osmanthus Branches"

Wang Anshi

I look toward the fallen land
of our nation, old capital,
where the only thing that hasn't changed

is the first chill of late autumn.

The river remains
a strand of glossed silk

ruling the interminable green peaks that rise
like regimented arrowheads.

Flags at the taverns slant in the west wind.

Boats sail into sunset,
crossing the vast reflections of clouds.
White egrets
lift their wings, distant, trembling like stars.

No ink-wash painting can capture what I see.
I think of the old times,

when the dignitaries and royalty
competed lavishly, constructing ostentatious
towers and palaces that became
witnesses to a continuum of tragedies.

For the last thousand years, how many poets
have climbed up here, sighing
the shame and glory of their own countries?

The histories of Six Dynasties vanished
along the rushing water.

Only the mist remains
above the river, and the dew continues
forming on grass.

Song girls continue
singing on the other bank of the river.

The same song that once ended a kingdom.

Solitude

卜算子·黄州定慧院寓居作

苏轼

缺月挂疏桐，漏断人初静。
谁见幽人独往来，缥缈孤鸿影。

惊起却回头，有恨无人省。
拣尽寒枝不肯栖，寂寞沙洲冷。

At the Dinghui Temple in Huangzhou

To the Tune "Bu Suan Zi: Calculating the Future"

Su Shi

The crescent slung on the bare boughs of a sycamore tree.
    The water clock stops. Human quiet.
    A quietness that is not for men.

Have you seen the soul arrested in grief and solitude pacing
    in his own shadow like a lost goose?
    I turn back to find this grief touched by no one.

The goose doesn't settle on any branch of the sycamore,
    flying across the sand dunes
    cooling in moonlight—vast cold with no end.

忆王孙·春词

李重元

萋萋芳草忆王孙。柳外楼高空断魂。
杜宇声声不忍闻。欲黄昏。雨打梨花深闭门。

Lyrics in Spring

To the Tune "Yi Wang Sun: Memories of the Royal Princes"

Li Chongyuan

Feeding on memories,
the scented herbage proliferates.

Tall willows. The pavilion emptied of crowds
is a body without its soul.

All day the delirious cuckoo sighs,
Come back, come back.

Near dusk. Rain pelts the pear blossoms hard.
I close the doors.

武陵春・春晚

李清照

风住尘香花已尽，日晚倦梳头。
物是人非事事休，欲语泪先流。

闻说双溪春尚好，也拟泛轻舟。
只恐双溪舴艋舟，载不动许多愁。

Spring Ends

To the Tune "Wu Ling Chun: Springtime at Wu Ling"

Li Qingzhao

Wind halts—the dust fragrant
with disheveled petals.

Evening—I am too tired
to comb my hair.

Things—remain;
people—gone. Everything

has come to an end.
Tears come before words.

I heard at the Twin Streams
the spring remains

ravishing. I thought of going,
spending the night

on a light boat. But I fear
those grasshopper boats

could not bear so much sorrow.

浣溪沙

李清照

小院闲窗春色深，重帘未卷影沉沉。
倚楼无语理瑶琴。

远岫出云催薄暮，细风吹雨弄轻阴。
梨花欲谢恐难禁。

To the Tune "Huan Xi Sha: Silk-Washing Brook"

Li Qingzhao

My little courtyard
deep in the deep

current of spring.
The curtains unrolled,

the room heavy
with shadows.

I sit quietly,
tuning the zither.

The far peaks
deliver the clouds

like a message
that asks for

another veil of rain
before dusk.

This evening,
I am so afraid I cannot

keep the pear blossoms
from shriveling.

摊破浣溪沙

李清照

病起萧萧两鬓华，卧看残月上窗纱。
豆蔻连梢煎熟水，莫分茶。

枕上诗书闲处好，门前风景雨来佳。
终日向人多酝藉，木犀花。

To the Tune "Tan Po Huan Xi Sha: Variation on Silk-Washing Brook"

Li Qingzhao

After illness: my earlocks
are blemished

with another shade of frost.
Through the gauze,

the moon waning.
I boil the cardamom seeds

along with their twigs.
There's no need for two cups.

I read poetry in bed.
Rain paints the view lovelier

outside my doorstep.
All day, the only benevolence

I receive comes from
the osmanthus blossoms.

添字丑奴儿

李清照

窗前谁种芭蕉树，阴满中庭。
阴满中庭。叶叶心心，舒卷有馀清。

伤心枕上三更雨，点滴霖霪。
点滴霖霪。愁损北人，不惯起来听。

To the Tune "Tian Zi Chou Nü Er: Variation on Ugly Doll"

Li Qingzhao

Who planted that banana tree
before my window? Its shadow brimming

my courtyard. My courtyard
under its huge shadow. Each leaf curls

about the sprout like a slim hand
clasping a heart. Heartbroken

on my pillow, and then this midnight rain.
Each raindrop batting a leaf.

Each leaf takes the raindrops in.
It saddens this woman from the north,

who is not used to the sorrow
of this southern night. What can she do?

Get up and listen quietly until dawn.

踏莎行・郴州旅舍

秦观

雾失楼台，月迷津渡。桃源望断无寻处。
可堪孤馆闭春寒，杜鹃声里斜阳暮。

驿寄梅花，鱼传尺素。砌成此恨无重数。
郴江幸自绕郴山，为谁流下潇湘去。

At a Hotel in Chenzhou

To the Tune "Ta Suo Xing: Treading on Purple Nutsedge"

Qin Guan

Those high balconies disappeared in fog.
The moon lost before the waterfront.
The Peach Blossom Spring
remains buried inside ancient scrolls.

Chill arrives early at this hotel
where the sun slants in the voice of cuckoos.
Horses rush to me, dappled
with plum blossoms from the post stop.

Silk letters found inside the slim guts of fish.
Sadness piles up. Chen Stream surrounds
Chen Mountain. Why does it
flow eastward, becoming River Xiaoxiang?

天仙子

张先

水调数声持酒听，午醉醒来愁未醒。
送春春去几时回。
临晚镜，伤流景，往事后期空记省。

沙上并禽池上暝，云破月来花弄影。
重重帘幕密遮灯。
风不定，人初静，明日落红应满径。

To the Tune "Tian Xian Zi: Goddess"

Zhang Xian

With a pot of rice wine, I listen
to the Tune of Water. After a noon nap,

my mind is sober; my sorrow is not.
How many more months till another springtime?

At this dim-lit hour, I take out the mirror.
My face is a floating arena of many yesterdays.

After dark, coupled wood ducks
drowsing at the pond's edge. Thin moonlight

cuts through clouds to emblazon the blossoms,
whose small thumbs ply their shadows.

Curtains withholding the lamplight.
Wind hasn't stopped yet, people silent with darkness.

The stone lanes shall turn crimson tomorrow,
buried under the fallen petals.

玉蝴蝶

柳永

望处雨收云断，凭阑悄悄，目送秋光。
晚景萧疏，堪动宋玉悲凉。
水风轻，蘋花渐老，月露冷、梧叶飘黄。
遣情伤。故人何在，烟水茫茫。

难忘，文期酒会，几孤风月，屡变星霜。
海阔山遥，未知何处是潇湘。
念双燕、难凭远信，指暮天、空识归航。
黯相望。断鸿声里，立尽斜阳。

To the Tune "Yu Hu Die: Jade Butterfly"

Liu Yong

Where the clouds break open, the rain ends.

I lean on the balustrade,
seeing off the last twilight of autumn sky.

This landscape bare and desolate
imitates the grievous phrases in Song Yu's poem.

The wind-damaged water pushes
the duckweed to age. The moon-chilled dew
bends sycamore trees to dark yellow.

Old friend, where are you?
Even the last fiber of your sleeves has dissolved
into clouds.

How could I forget
those banquets with inexhaustible rice wine and poetry.

And then, years
spent alone with the moon and the wind.

The shifting constellations that translate to frost
at my doorstep.

The broad sea is broad, and the mountains
insurmountable.
Even the paired swallows can't be trusted to carry
my letters to you.

How many times have I been lied to
by those returning boats

at the harbor
under a dusky sky? In the cries of wild geese,

I stand at the end of a slanted sun.

风入松

俞国宝

东风巷陌暮寒骄。灯火闹河桥。
胜游忆遍钱塘夜，青鸾远、信断难招。
蕙草情随雪尽，梨花梦与云销。

客怀先自病无聊。绿酒负金蕉。
下帏独拥香篝睡，春城外、玉漏声遥。
可惜满街明月，更无人为吹箫。

To the Tune "Feng Ru Song: Wind Passing Through Pines"

Yu Guobao

A tinge of cold in the streets brought by the east wind,
bridges bustling with lanterns and flames.
West Lake of yesterday, unreal as the blue phoenix.

Those primroses in love with the snow die
as the snow melts. Even the pear blossoms dream
of disentangling, those children of clouds.

At this foreign place, boredom is the worst illness.
A plate of bananas seems a terrible appetizer
for night drinking. In the guest room, I lie close

to the incense burner. Beyond the city gate, clepsydras
are remote but audible. Familiar moon
floods the avenue, but where's the flutist and her flute?

菩萨蛮

李清照

风柔日薄春犹早，夹衫乍著心情好。
睡起觉微寒，梅花鬓上残。

故乡何处是，忘了除非醉。
沉水卧时烧，香消酒未消。

To the Tune "Pu Sa Man: The Bodhisattva's Headdress"

Li Qingzhao

The breeze soft and sunlight faint
in days of early spring.

Light clothing too
puts me in a good mood. Waking up

from a nap, pricked by the cold's
needle—that stem of plum blossoms

on my hair broke a little.
Where is my homeland?

This nostalgia that thins out only
in my drunken dreams.

The incense burner I put on before my nap
has used up its fragrance.

Dreaming hasn't used up my drunkenness.

一剪梅

李清照

红藕香残玉簟秋。轻解罗裳，独上兰舟。
云中谁寄锦书来？雁字回时，月满西楼。

花自飘零水自流。一种相思，两处闲愁。
此情无计可消除，才下眉头，却上心头。

To the Tune "Yi Jian Mei: Snipping Plum Blossoms"

Li Qingzhao

Strong scent of lotuses dies away.
The bamboo mat
takes on the temperature of jade.

Unlacing my silk robe, I step on
the orchid boat.
Who'd send me a letter across clouds?

By the time the swans return,
the west pavilion
will become a deluge of moonlight.

The streamlet never slows down
for the floating petals.
One sorrow moors two distant hearts.

No way to cast aside this melancholy—
from the knot of my brows
it creeps up to the tip of my soul.

怨王孙·春暮

李清照

帝里春晚，重门深院。草绿阶前，暮天雁断。
楼上远信谁传，恨绵绵。

多情自是多沾惹，难拚舍，又是寒食也。
秋千巷陌，人静皎月初斜，浸梨花。

Late Spring

To the Tune "Yuan Wang Sun: A Complaint to My Young Lord"

Li Qingzhao

Spring late in the capital.
Behind heavy doors,

a shaded courtyard, grass grows
blue green before stairs.

In the dusky sky,
no trace of swans—who

would carry this letter for me?
Sorrow stretches

like new grass.
To love is to step on this grass.

Again, alone
on the Cold Food Festival.

The swings empty.
The lanes quiet,

as if no one lived.
The crescent, slanted, bright

with opalescent light,
soaking the pear blossoms.

好事近

李清照

风定落花深，帘外拥红堆雪。
长记海棠开后，正伤春时节。

酒阑歌罢玉尊空，青缸暗明灭。
魂梦不堪幽怨，更一声鶗鴂。

To the Tune "Hao Shi Jin: Fortunes Near"

Li Qingzhao

When the wind stops, the fallen flowers
pile up a broad carpet.
Beyond the veil, red petals lapping the snow.
After the blooming of crabapple trees
comes the usual spring sorrow.
The singing stops. The wine cups drain.
The night continues in emptiness.
A bead of fire flickers blue
in the bronze lamp. The dream
that gives sadness its shapes has already been
unbearable, let alone now a cuckoo's cry.

Unbridled

临江仙·夜归临皋

苏轼

夜饮东坡醒复醉，归来仿佛三更。
家童鼻息已雷鸣。敲门都不应，倚杖听江声。

长恨此身非我有，何时忘却营营。
夜阑风静縠纹平。小舟从此逝，江海寄余生。

Return to Lin Gao at Night

To the Tune "Lin Jiang Xian: Riverside Immortals"

Su Shi

Drunk at Eastern Slope, sober up, get drunk again.
When I return, it's past midnight.
I hear the servant boy snoring behind the locked doors
and think there's a thunderstorm in my house.
No one answers my knocking.
Leaning on my bamboo cane,
all night I listen to the river repeating itself to itself.
I hate that this body is not my body
and my life not mine. When can I forget about
chasing after fortune and fame like a frenetic donkey?
Darkness deepens. The wind straightens
the water it has made crooked.
An empty boat vanishing into the night.
To the rivers and the sea I shall tether the rest of my life.

贺新郎

辛弃疾

甚矣吾衰矣。
怅平生、交游零落，只今余几！
白发空垂三千丈，一笑人间万事。
问何物、能令公喜？
我见青山多妩媚，料青山见我应如是。
情与貌，略相似。

一尊搔首东窗里。
想渊明、停云诗就，此时风味。
江左沉酣求名者，岂识浊醪妙理。
回首叫、云飞风起。
不恨古人吾不见，恨古人不见吾狂耳。
知我者，二三子。

To the Tune "He Xin Lang: Toasting the Bridegroom"

Xin Qiji

Now that I am old, those who crossed the mountains and oceans
with me are parts of the mountains and oceans.
I still call those dirty skeletons: my friends.
My friends, now that my white hair is thirty thousand feet long,
taking up so much room around me, nothing in this life
can't be concluded with a laugh—all those infatuated dreams
of fruitless desire, years in the military, and my ambition
in politics to serve my nation since youth, all these are like the porridge
dumped into a slop bucket. What can make me happy? What
has ever made me happy? Suddenly, I recognize the blue mountains
as dashing and handsome; didn't know all the while
the blue mountains thought the same about me. After all, we look similar—
the same wrinkly crags and cliffs, mosses and mustaches,
and now, the same stone heart we share.
Holding a pot of wine, I scratch my head at the east-side window,
wondering if Tao Yuanming felt the same after he finished his poem
about the halted clouds. What do those politicians
delirious at the left bank of the Yangtze understand about the true nature
of drinking—their feet in sewage, fishing feverish dreams

of fame and money? I turn to holler at the empty landscape,
to startle the clouds and the storm's surges.
I don't feel sorry that I can't meet those dead
ancient poets. Instead, I feel sorry for them
not being able to drink with me, a man writ large, unbridled and wild.
Friends, I am understood only by the mountains, your buried bones.

丑奴儿·书博山道中壁

辛弃疾

少年不识愁滋味，爱上层楼。
爱上层楼，为赋新词强说愁。

而今识尽愁滋味，欲说还休。
欲说还休，却道天凉好个秋。

Written on a Wall in Boshan
To the Tune "Chou Nü Er: Ugly Doll"

Xin Qiji

When I was young, I knew
nothing about sorrow. Still, I loved
going up the high tower. Up
on the high tower, I wrote poems
with my imagined sorrow.

Now that I've tasted every
bite of sorrow, I want to spit it out;
I can't. Having chosen
to reside with silence, I say:
This autumn day is cool and beautiful.

丑奴儿

辛弃疾

烟迷露麦荒池柳，洗雨烘晴。
洗雨烘晴，一样春风几样青。

提壶脱袴催归去，万恨千情。
万恨千情，各自无聊各自鸣。

To the Tune "Chou Nü Er: Ugly Doll"

Xin Qiji

The fog lifts above the lakes
while dew settles on the abandoned wheat fields.
The rain came, then the sun. The sun,
then the rain. The spring
wind ruffling all tints of green at once.

I pick up my flagon and robe
to return home. So many feelings in my heart.
In everyone's heart, too many
feelings. In this world, people
have nothing to do, each making a sound.

西江月·遣兴

辛弃疾

醉里且贪欢笑，要愁那得工夫。
近来始觉古人书，信著全无是处。

昨夜松边醉倒，问松我醉何如。
只疑松动要来扶，以手推松曰去！

Amusement

To the Tune "Xi Jiang Yue: West River Moon"

Xin Qiji

When I'm drunk, I feel happier,
have no time to get sad.
I recently discovered those great tomes
by ancient saints are not
only boring but basically hogwash.

Last night I drank beside a pine tree.
I asked the pine tree, *Guess*
how drunk I am. It swayed in the wind
as if coming to hold me.
I pushed it away and said, *Piss off!*

渔家傲

李清照

天接云涛连晓雾，星河欲转千帆舞。
仿佛梦魂归帝所。闻天语，殷勤问我归何处。

我报路长嗟日暮，学诗谩有惊人句。
九万里风鹏正举。风休住，蓬舟吹取三山去！

To the Tune "Yu Jia Ao: Pride of Fishermen"

Li Qingzhao

Fused with tides of clouds, the bluish horizon emerges
from dawn's mist, and constellations
pirouette like a thousand sails quaking in a tempest.

My soul seems to have returned to before birth,
to the palace of the Emperor of Heaven,
who asks me gently, Tell me, my daughter, to where
are you traversing so restlessly with this life and dream?

I replied that the path is long
and infinite, and now already, the sundown.

What do all those years of studying poetry count for?
What is one splendid line compared to a rice stalk
that can save children one night in this fire, famine, and war.

Now that the phoenix queen unfolds her vast feathers
and travels ninety thousand miles a day.

Wind, do not stop, keep rising, carry this leaf of boat away
from this world to the Three Mountains.

行香子·述怀

苏轼

清夜无尘，月色如银。
酒斟时、须满十分。浮名浮利，虚苦劳神。
叹隙中驹，石中火，梦中身。

虽抱文章，开口谁亲。
且陶陶、乐尽天真。几时归去，作个闲人。
对一张琴，一壶酒，一溪云。

Expression

To the Tune "Xing Xiang Zi: Walk Through Incense Smoke"

Su Shi

The clear night speckless, the moon silvering.
Tonight, wine must be poured
till it overflows the bronze cup.

This continuous quest for worldly goods and fame
that grinds my soul.
Time flees like a stable of white steeds.

This body enclosed by false dreams
is a stone surrounded by fire.

Who could bring back my innocence,
make me useless? For whom,
I keep thinning my waist to fatten my poetry?

A zither, a pot of wine,
reflection of clouds erasing parts of the creek.

满庭芳

苏轼

蜗角虚名，蝇头微利，算来著甚干忙。
事皆前定，谁弱又谁强。
且趁闲身未老，尽放我、些子疏狂。
百年里，浑教是醉，三万六千场。

思量。能几许，忧愁风雨，一半相妨。
又何须抵死，说短论长。
幸对清风皓月，苔茵展、云幕高张。
江南好，千钟美酒，一曲满庭芳。

To the Tune "Man Ting Fang: Courtyard Blossoms"

Su Shi

What are you all still fighting for?
Heads broken, hands at one another's throat
for that vain crown of fame
like a snail's horns, with profits negligible
like heads of fruit flies.
Who gets ahead, who gets behind—who
cares? Before this body gets ravaged
by time, you can still fill your hundred years
on earth with wine and legless drunkenness
thirty-six thousand more times.
Think about it, half your life was buried
behind the tragic form of storms.
Why keep comparing the short with long,
right with wrong till death
knocks on your crispy forehead?
Now the breeze is clear and the moon bright,
and the moss emerald
stretches like an enormous tapestry to meet
the canopy of clouds. South
of the Yangtze remains a great place—
a thousand pots of wine, a song that drives
all buds in the courtyard to full blossoming.

风入松

俞国宝

一春长费买花钱，日日醉湖边。
玉骢惯识西湖路，骄嘶过、沽酒楼前。
红杏香中箫鼓，绿杨影里秋千。

暖风十里丽人天，花压鬓云偏。
画船载取春归去，馀情寄、湖水湖烟。
明日重扶残醉，来寻陌上花钿。

To the Tune "Feng Ru Song: Wind Passing Through Pines"

Yu Guobao

Since spring, I have lost count of how much money
I spent at the flower market, every day
drunk at the lakeside. My jade-white horse
knows ways around West Lake
better than I, neighing past the wine stores
and taverns, past a crowd of drums
and bamboo flutes, and the loud apricot blossoms
where the swing moves silently
in the long shadow of poplar trees. The wind
warm as the breath of a fair maiden,
whose dark tresses are lit darker by a bright flower.
The painted boat returns carrying
another April sunset, while our hearts are left
with smoke on the lake water.
Tomorrow, let me hold up this body again, staggering
with leftover tipsiness to find the hairpin
lost on the footpath, to end up repeating yesterday.

采桑子

欧阳修

画船载酒西湖好，急管繁弦，玉盏催传，稳泛平波任醉眠。
行云却在行舟下，空水澄鲜，俯仰留连，疑是湖中别有天。

To the Tune "Cai Sang Zi: Picking Mulberries"

Ouyang Xiu

How great to get a long sleep
on the painted boat loaded with wine
on West Lake.
The musicians pulling the melodies
from the pipes
and the sound of cups clinking
and oars lapping the waves
softly, softly. Clouds
float beneath our moving boat.
The lake is transparent, another heaven.

西江月・平山堂

苏轼

三过平山堂下，半生弹指声中。
十年不见老仙翁，壁上龙蛇飞动。

欲吊文章太守，仍歌杨柳春风。
休言万事转头空，未转头时皆梦。

At Pingshan Temple

To the Tune "Xi Jiang Yue: West River Moon"

Su Shi

It's the third time I pass by Pingshan Hall.
Half of my life went by with a snap
of the fingers. My teacher, Ouyang Xiu,
has been dead for ten years.
After ten years, his cursive calligraphy remains
breathing on the walls like a dragon
slaughtering a battalion of snakes.
I am supposed to come and write an elegy
to memorialize his literary legacy.
Instead, I insist on singing
about the poplars and willows in the spring breeze.
Don't say that whenever you turn back,
everything becomes emptiness.
What's ahead of you remains an illusion.

望江南·超然台作

苏轼

春未老，风细柳斜斜。
试上超然台上看，半壕春水一城花。
烟雨暗千家。

寒食后，酒醒却咨嗟。
休对故人思故国，且将新火试新茶。
诗酒趁年华。

At Transcendent Terrace

To the Tune "Wang Jiangnan: Longing for Jiangnan"

Su Shi

Spring hasn't grown old yet.
Willows lean diagonal in the lanky breeze.

Overlooking from Transcendent Terrace—
the moat half full with green water.

Beside the roads edged with flowers,
a thousand households turn dim in the misty rain.

After the Cold Food Festival, I wake up
to a veil of unspeakable nostalgia.

Why bother to keep babbling
old days to an old friend. Start a fresh fire
to brew the freshly picked tea leaves.

Come, get drunk. Our best years
have yet to be poured into lines of poetry.

念奴娇·过洞庭

张孝祥

洞庭青草，近中秋，更无一点风色。
玉鉴琼田三万顷，着我扁舟一叶。
素月分辉，明河共影，表里俱澄澈。
悠然心会，妙处难与君说。

应念岭海经年，孤光自照，肝肺皆冰雪。
短发萧骚襟袖冷，稳泛沧浪空阔。
尽挹西江，细斟北斗，万象为宾客。
扣舷独啸，不知今夕何夕。

Passing Dong Ting Lake

To the Tune "Nian Nü Jiao: Remembering the Singing Lady"

Zhang Xiaoxiang

At Dong Ting, the glasslike grasses
seem an extension of the lake. There isn't a trace of wind
on the Moon Festival; everything is kept
to itself. The lake water burnished
like a giant mirror and the boundless rice fields ripening
into maroon gemstones, and among them I ride on a wood raft,
like a leaf crossing the quiet color of the moon,
beside which the bright galaxy pours
a torrent from heaven wetting the lake stars. My heart
seems to be made of that lucid water,
a clarity inside me that words cannot display.
Thinking about my youthful years working in the remote
areas of Lingnan, alone with the same moonlight
that had filled my lungs and liver with frosted ice.
Now that I'm old, with shaved hair and thin clothing, I feel
a vastness inside me. Let me pour empty
the West River as wine, use the Big Dipper as a ladle
and invite all worldly things as my guests.
The world is just a passing guest of my mind. Alone I strum
my zither and sing, forgetting what year it is,
while time keeps passing through my body, so time lives.

Nostalgia

临江仙·夜登小阁忆洛中旧游

陈与义

忆昔午桥桥上饮，坐中多是豪英。
长沟流月去无声。杏花疏影里，吹笛到天明。

二十余年如一梦，此身虽在堪惊。
闲登小阁看新晴。古今多少事，渔唱起三更。

On the Tower at Midnight

To the Tune "Lin Jiang Xian: Riverside Immortals"

Chen Yuyi

I still remember drinking on the Bridge of Noon
with the best minds of my generation.

The reflection of moon lay quietly in the ditch,
and the flowing water could not move it.

In the sparse shade of apricot blossoms,
someone was playing the flute until the dawn hour.

Twenty years went by like a dream.
To think that I am still alive gives me cold sweats.

The sky clears at the pavilion. How many
palaces rise and fall in history? Those skeletons

of heroes who come alive at midnight
as faint melodies on the fisherman's chapped lips.

念奴娇·赤壁怀古

苏轼

大江东去，浪淘尽，千古风流人物。
故垒西边，人道是，三国周郎赤壁。
乱石穿空，惊涛拍岸，卷起千堆雪。江山如画，一时多少豪杰。

遥想公瑾当年，小乔初嫁了，雄姿英发。
羽扇纶巾，谈笑间，樯橹灰飞烟灭。
故国神游，多情应笑我，早生华发。人生如梦，一尊还酹江月。

Meditation at the Red Cliff

To the Tune "Nian Nü Jiao: Remembering the Singing Lady"

Su Shi

The waves of a vast river running
ceaselessly eastward have swept away the heroic figures
of the last thousand years. At the west of the fortress,
so the tale goes, once stood General Zhou Yu
of the Three Kingdoms. At the Red Cliff,
the air was sliced by thrusts of flying rocks, the roaring
in the soldiers' chests becoming floods that smashed open
crags and cliffs on the shoreline,
rolling into a thousand heaves of snow.
The rivers and mountains were like a painting,
slowly assembling under the heroes' broad hands.
Right after his wedding, General Zhou Yu,
at the age of twenty-four, handsome, already valorous.
Wearing a silken cap, holding a feather fan,
talking and laughing, he put his enemies' ships
and fortress to ashes and smoke.
I like dreaming of those dead kingdoms
and shall be laughed at for my heart of high romance,
my beard white as the froth on the shore. This life
floats like a waking dream. I pour empty this jar of wine,
a libation to the moon motionless on the river.

苏幕遮·怀旧

范仲淹

碧云天，黄叶地，秋色连波，波上寒烟翠。
山映斜阳天接水，芳草无情，更在斜阳外。

黯乡魂，追旅思，夜夜除非，好梦留人睡。
明月楼高休独倚，酒入愁肠，化作相思泪。

Nostalgia

To the Tune "Su Mu Zhe: Water-Splaying"

Fan Zhongyan

Turquoise sky, field covered with yellow leaves,
and where autumn colors merge
with lake tides, the mist hangs faint emerald.

Mountains washed red in sunset.
Scented herbs stretching beyond the twilight's
touch are the bitterest, cruelest.

Years on the road, with a soul burning
to repeat my hometown in sleep. Uncounted nights,
even sweet dreams fail to keep me in bed.

The rice wine coursing through my sorrowful
bowel becomes tears for the past.
Moon rises. Don't lean on the high tower alone.

水龙吟·登建康赏心亭

辛弃疾

楚天千里清秋，水随天去秋无际。
遥岑远目，献愁供恨，玉簪螺髻。
落日楼头，断鸿声里，江南游子。
把吴钩看了，栏干拍遍，无人会，登临意。

休说鲈鱼堪脍，尽西风，季鹰归未？
求田问舍，怕应羞见，刘郎才气。
可惜流年，忧愁风雨，树犹如此！
倩何人唤取，红巾翠袖，揾英雄泪！

At the Shangxin Pavilion, Jiankang
To the Tune "Shui Long Yin: Water Dragon Chants"
Xin Qiji

A clear autumn evening in the State of Chu. The lake water
meets with the sky, multiplying the spareness.
Wherever I look, those peaks and summits arranged
like treasurable conches, or like plaited chignons
with emerald hairpins—all possessions of the enemy.
The setting sun pauses a second for the shrill
of wild geese. I pause from examining my dagger
to keep climbing the tower. Who would know
my agony with such a landscape in my eyes? I knock against
the railings repeatedly, till the hills darken.

For centuries, Jiying of the West Jin was praised for resigning
his official post, because the striped bass
in his hometown were fat and in season. Is that a luxury
of peacetime? A home to return to? Fussy delicacy?
Well, I'm deposed, living in a village, all day caring
about land prices and the real estate market
for personal comfort. Should I be ashamed? Time abrades
me into complete uselessness, like this country

in the ceaseless storms. Who would come to my side now,
    in green sleeves with a pink handkerchief,
wiping off tears of a robbed hero? Even the tree has grown
    and withered—what can you ask of a man?

摸鱼儿

辛弃疾

更能消、几番风雨，匆匆春又归去。
惜春长怕花开早，何况落红无数!
春且住。
见说道，天涯芳草无归路。
怨春不语。
算只有殷勤，画檐蛛网，尽日惹飞絮。

长门事，准拟佳期又误。
蛾眉曾有人妒。
千金纵买相如赋，脉脉此情谁诉?
君莫舞。
君不见，玉环飞燕皆尘土!
闲愁最苦。
休去倚危栏，斜阳正在，烟柳断肠处。

To the Tune "Mo Yu Er: Prodding Fish"

Xin Qiji

How many more rainstorms can you still endure, spring—
now that you are leaving again, too soon.

Now I am old, afraid of those flowers,
whipped warm by wind, blooming too early, let alone that the sky
is veiled with specks of drifting red
petals and earth with countless dropped red.

Spring, can't you see that the infinite sweep
of blossoms and fragrant meadows is closing off your road?
Under the glazed roof tiles the spiderwebs
assiduously collect a bowl of petals, shreds of you.

✦

All because someone was envious of her exquisite eyebrows—
Empress Chen, deposed at Long Gate,
spent crates of gold
imploring Xiangru to write a love poem pleading
for the return of a man's heart.
But who would listen to such lasting affection?

Or how Empress Zhao and Consort Yang were bestowed
a strand of silk rope
to hang themselves—a fallen nation weighing upon
their tenuous waists—
supervised by the emperors' attendants.
But then, who said they weren't once loved?

Please, do not dance.
Can't you see those who had danced are now dust?

But then, this life is safe and wasted
without dancing—I lean on the balustrade as if a broken rag.

The dusk casts a soft light over the willows,
mist-shrouded, looking like a tree line of guts torn to pieces.

梅花引・荆溪阻雪

蒋捷

白鸥问我泊孤舟，是身留，是心留？
心若留时，何事锁眉头？
风拍小帘灯晕舞，对闲影，冷清清，忆旧游。

旧游旧游今在否？花外楼，柳下舟。
梦也梦也，梦不到，寒水空流。
漠漠黄云，湿透木棉裘。
都道无人愁似我，今夜雪，有梅花，似我愁。

Stuck in a Snowstorm at Jin Stream
To the Tune "Mei Hua Yin: Prelude of Plum Blossoms"

Jiang Jie

Are you trapped here, the white gull asks me
while I moor my boat, or are you leaving behind your heart?

If your heart is left behind,
what keeps twisting your eyebrows like a lock?
Wind flaps the boat curtain, bending a wisp of fishing lamp.

Old days, old days, how have you left me—
pavilion beyond pear blossoms, canoe beneath wild willows.

I dream and dream and dream
and at the dream's end—cold river runs emptily.
Clouds muddy, colossal.

Snow dampens my red cotton clothes.
The plum blossoms open in the exact shape of my sorrow.

望海潮・洛阳怀古

秦观

梅英疏淡，冰澌溶泄，东风暗换年华。
金谷俊游，铜驼巷陌，新晴细履平沙。长记误随车。
正絮翻蝶舞，芳思交加。柳下桃蹊，乱分春色到人家。

西园夜饮鸣笳。有华灯碍月，飞盖妨花。
兰苑未空，行人渐老，重来是事堪嗟。烟暝酒旗斜。
但倚楼极目，时见栖鸦。无奈归心，暗随流水到天涯。

Nostalgia at Luoyang

To the Tune "Wang Hai Chao: Watching the Sea Tides"

Qin Guan

As ice leaks in strings of water,
the scent of plum blossoms grows thin.

Overnight, east wind redecorates the landscape.

Remember touring the Golden Valley,
the bells ringing as the copper camels strolled past,
heard ten blocks away.
Our shoes raising mild dust.

Butterflies cut across veils
of cotton fluff, parceling specks of spring
colors to households.

Remember drinking at the West Garden,
music of reed pipes.

The florid lamps eclipsing the moon,
and tents blocked away too many drifting petals.

Now that I revisit this old place,
the garden manages to preserve the summertime,
leaving winter growing in my hair.

The banner of a tavern slants in the morning fog.

Ducks resting on their edge of water.
I envy them.

How come this heart, heavy
with homesickness, is carried again by the restless
water to the earth's end?

八声甘州・灵岩陪庾幕诸公游

吴文英

渺空烟四远，是何年、青天坠长星？
幻苍崖云树，名娃金屋，残霸宫城。
箭径酸风射眼，腻水染花腥。时靸双鸳响，廊叶秋声。

宫里吴王沉醉，倩五湖倦客，独钓醒醒。
问苍波无语，华发奈山青。
水涵空、阑干高处，送乱鸦斜日落渔汀。
连呼酒、上琴台去，秋与云平。

Visiting Lingyan Mountain

To the Tune "Ba Sheng Ganzhou: Eight Rhymes of Ganzhou"

Wu Wenying

Mist unfolds to all sides: what year: since a comet fell
from heaven: darkening cerulean: so that conceived: this
escarpment that impends: trees knotted with clouds:
so that upon which: this ruin: once the magnificent palace
of the king of Wu: where the deadly beauty of Xi Shi
was concealed: so that in this arrow-shaped passageway:
whetted wind darting my eyes: and rivers coated
with grease from rouge: made of pomegranate, camellia,
safflower, and sappanwood: sodden blossoms
ravishing on the riverbanks: reek like day-old blood:
years past: pine needles in the corridor: echo the footsteps in clogs:

For this square-sized luxury: the king of Wu: surrenders rivers
and mountains of the nation: leaving
the literati to their uninhabited lakeside: their minds still vigilant
as a fishing rod above water: speechless
water: explains the rising and falling: of an empire it witnessed
by showing me: my white hair against the black
mountain ridge: immovable water: where the sky lives a second
time: crows descend on the slant ladder of sun:
bring more wine: it is still not too late to go to Zither Terrace:
the last autumn light leveled with the clouds:

高阳台・落梅

吴文英

宫粉雕痕，仙云堕影，无人野水荒湾。
古石埋香，金沙锁骨连环。南楼不恨吹横笛，恨晓风、千里关山。
半飘零，庭上黄昏，月冷阑干。

寿阳空理愁鸾。问谁调玉髓，暗补香瘢。
细雨归鸿，孤山无限春寒。离魂难倩招清些，梦缟衣、解佩溪边。
最愁人，啼鸟清明，叶底青圆。

Ode to Falling Plum Blossoms

To the Tune "Gao Yang Tai: Sun Terrace"

Wu Wenying

Descension: flake off
like the ivory powder from a concubine's
nose ridge in the depths

of the Forbidden Palace: or that gauze sash
of an immortal slipping
through clouds: in search of the uncharted water

at a dreamed-up sandbank:
scented clavicles:
identical to the interlocked emerald bracelets
buried beneath gold dust:

hate not the flute from the South Tower:
hate the boreal wind

crossing hills ten-thousandfold: at dawn hour:
so this descension: flakes of white

midair: dusk in the palm of the courtyard:
balustrade rime frosted in moonlight:

✦

Princess Shouyang who is said to be an orphan
of Plum-Blossom God
now sets her face to the mirror's assailment:

whose patient hands would grind
the chalcedony into pallid powder to mend:
cinquefoil bruises

on her forehead: watermarked
by the fallen petals: swan geese in lean rain:

doors of mountain
withholding the last coldness of spring:

gone apparition: how can you be coaxed
into reappearing
in the dream's short creek:

untie the jade pendent from your cerecloth:
untie the jade pendent from your cerecloth:

mourning is not to recall the birds' callous
singing: but living to witness:

beneath the crammed green
of leaves: plums already pellucid, round, lasting:

临江仙

晏几道

梦后楼台高锁，酒醒帘幕低垂。
去年春恨却来时。落花人独立，微雨燕双飞。

记得小蘋初见，两重心字罗衣。琵琶弦上说相思。
当时明月在，曾照彩云归。

To the Tune "Lin Jiang Xian: Riverside Immortals"

YAN JIDAO

Dreams end, pavilions locked up.
Sober up, curtains unrolled.
How to describe spring sorrow again?

Alone, amid falling petals.
Swallows flit past a sheet of light rain.

When we first met, you wore
a heart-patterned dress,
confiding lovesickness on strings of the pipa.

Once the moon was bright,
sending off that wisp of glazed clouds.

一剪梅

无名氏

漠漠春阴酒半酣。风透春衫，雨透春衫。
人家蚕事欲眠三。桑满筐篮，柘满筐篮。

先自离怀百不堪。樯燕呢喃，梁燕呢喃。
篝灯强把锦书看。人在江南，心在江南。

To the Tune "Yi Jian Mei: Snipping Plum Blossoms"

Anonymous

Late spring, drizzle moistens my thin clothing.
    My clothing cooling in the breeze.

This afternoon, I will feed my silkworms
    with a basket of mulberry leaves
    and a basket of melon-berry leaves.

I will listen to the swallows on the beam.
    Swallows on the mast.

I will light all the candles to read your letter
    after dark—I am not in Jiangnan,
    I am nowhere but Jiangnan.

Passing Years

永遇乐

李清照

落日熔金，暮云合璧，人在何处。
染柳烟浓，吹梅笛怨，春意知几许。
元宵佳节，融和天气，次第岂无风雨。
来相召、香车宝马，谢他酒朋诗侣。

中州盛日，闺门多暇，记得偏重三五。
铺翠冠儿，撚金雪柳，簇带争济楚。
如今憔悴，风鬟霜鬓，怕见夜间出去。
不如向、帘儿底下，听人笑语。

To the Tune "Yong Yu Le: Everlasting Joy"

Li Qingzhao

The sunset an incinerated scrap of gold,
clouds darkening like jade shards, broken then mended.

You, who survived the war and disasters,
where are you?

Fog rises, smudging willows' deep green,
and the plum petals
drop like notes flying off a flute.

Do you still remember how to be happy in springtime?

It's the Lantern Festival, the weather
falsely pleasant—
we need a storm to snatch us back to reality.

Friends came with wine and poetry
in their splendid carriages, inviting me to a banquet.
I thanked them and chose to stay home.

I think of the time in Zhongzhou,
during the Lantern Festival, girls wearing emerald circlets,
or the sumptuous headdresses
braided with gold threads called Willow in Snow.

Now that I've aged, ravaged,
my hair the color of dandelion fuzz,

I'm afraid to go to the night bazaars. It's better to hide

behind those heavy curtains
and listen intently
to strangers laughing, talking away the night.

唐多令

刘过

芦叶满汀洲，寒沙带浅流。
二十年重过南楼。
柳下系船犹未稳，能几日，又中秋。

黄鹤断矶头，故人今在否？
旧江山浑是新愁。
欲买桂花同载酒，终不似，少年游。

To the Tune "Tang Duo Ling: A Little Song"

Liu Guo

Reed leaves pile on the shoal, sand dented
with streamlines of waves.

Twenty years later, I return
to the South Tower, leaving the oarsman

to tie the boat to a willow.
In a few days, Mid-Autumn Festival.

At Yellow Crane Tower,
the rugged coastline brackish and eroded.

Are my friends the same way?
Old mountains filled with new sorrow.

I'm thinking of buying
osmanthus branches and wine, to invite you

for drinks on the lake. But then, why bother?
We are not who we were.

点绛唇

李清照

蹴罢秋千，起来慵整纤纤手。
露浓花瘦，薄汗轻衣透。

见客入来，袜刬金钗溜。
和羞走，倚门回首，却把青梅嗅。

To the Tune "Dian Jiang Chun: Rouged Lips"

Li Qingzhao

Getting off the swing,
she rubs her hands

mindlessly. Dew heavy
on the desiccated

petals. Light sweat
dampens her diaphanous

lapel. When a guest enters
the yard, she hurries

to hide—her silk sock
slips off, along with a gold

hairpin. She leans
behind a pillar, blushing,

pretending to sniff
a twig of green plums.

少年游

周邦彦

并刀如水，吴盐胜雪，纤手破新橙。
锦幄初温，兽烟不断，相对坐调笙。

低声问：向谁行宿？城上已三更。
马滑霜浓，不如休去，直是少人行！

To the Tune "Shao Nian You: Youthful Excursion"

Zhou Bangyan

On the table, scissors from Bing Province
polished more pellucid than water.

Beside this bowl of salt from south of the Yangtze,
even snow would lose its gleam.

Her slim hands slit open a tangerine.
The damask curtains just getting warm

from the vapor of the incense burner, looking
like a bronze animal crunching the air.

We sit facing each other, tuning up our reed pipe
instruments. In a low-pitched

whisper, she said to me: It's getting late.
The frost is thick, and the road too slippery

for the horses. So few people would go outside.
Why don't you stay the night?

满庭芳·促织儿

张镃

月洗高梧，露漙幽草，宝钗楼外秋深。
土花沿翠，萤火坠墙阴。
静听寒声断续，微韵转、凄咽悲沉。
争求侣，殷勤劝织，促破晓机心。

儿时，曾记得，呼灯灌穴，敛步随音。
任满身花影，犹自追寻。
携向华堂戏斗，亭台小、笼巧妆金。
今休说，从渠床下，凉夜伴孤吟。

Cricket
To the Tune "Man Ting Fang: Courtyard Blossoms"

Zhang Zi

Outside the Golden Hairpin Attic—tall sycamore trees,
moon-basked, grasses ignited in silver, rounded
with dew—autumn deepens. Where the lichen slouches,
glowworms plunge to the corner of a stone wall.
The coarse screech of crickets, night's maudlin tautology,
has the rhythm of my mother's spinning wheel,
which once urged her repeating hands to keep
repeating—my childhood—I remember—with a lantern
in my hands and a jug of clear water—I remember—following
the crickets' song, tiptoeing through the dankest mud—
I remember—despite the dense shadow of flowers
weighing down my slim shoulders, all night I kept chasing
their voices till morning—morning, I brought their thin,
trembling bodies for fights at the marketplace,
where the cricket boxes, so delicate, gilded like little pagodas,
were strapped around the boys' waists. Now that I am sick
and dying, alone in this dilapidated cottage,
the crickets come to sing under my bed frame—
frigid hours, sustained by the crickets' song . . . I start singing.

鹧鸪天·有客慨然谈功名因追念少年时事戏作

辛弃疾

壮岁旌旗拥万夫，锦襜突骑渡江初。
燕兵夜娖银胡簶，汉箭朝飞金仆姑。

追往事，叹今吾，春风不染白髭须。
却将万字平戎策，换得东家种树书。

A Parody of My Recent Life
To the Tune "Zhe Gu Tian: Partridge Sky"

Xin Qiji

When I was young, I led ten thousand
soldiers crossing the Yangtze River overnight.
While the enemies were still filling
their quivers, our arrows attacked
like comets. Now I retire to a village,
a nobody. Not even spring wind can bring
back the black of my beard. That bulk
of stratagems I wrote to the court
on bringing back our lost land . . . Here
I am rewarded with this barren field, a bucket,
a mattock, and a book from a neighbor
in the east, titled *How to Grow Trees.*

虞美人·听雨

蒋捷

少年听雨歌楼上，红烛昏罗帐。
壮年听雨客舟中，江阔云低、断雁叫西风。

而今听雨僧庐下，鬓已星星也。
悲欢离合总无情，一任阶前、点滴到天明。

Listening to Rain

To the Tune "Yu Mei Ren: The Beautiful Lady Yu"

Jiang Jie

In my boyhood, I listened
to the rain at the lavish tower—melodies
and candle flames flicker
dimly across the gauze curtain.

In my adulthood, I listened
to the rain on a rootless boat,
clouds level with the inlet—a goose's shriek,
colder than the west wind.

Now I live at a monk's cottage—
my sideburns, star-stained.
My heart has changed.
Something is falling, drop by drop till dawn.

诉衷情

陆游

当年万里觅封侯，匹马戍梁州。
关河梦断何处？尘暗旧貂裘。

胡未灭，鬓先秋，泪空流。
此生谁料，心在天山，身老沧洲。

To the Tune "Su Zhong Qing: Telling My Heart"

Lu You

In the old days, I enlisted at the borderland,
guarding my people with one horse
and one sword. Those days reappear now
in my dream, where the frozen Guan River's
bone-piercing as half a century ago.
I wake up—my sable coat grows darkish
in dust. Enemies keep slaughtering my people.
But I am old, sick as a sycamore in fall.
All I have are these useless, weak tears.
Who would have thought: This life, my heart
never leaves the front line in Tian Shan,
my body paralyzed in this hut at Cangzhou.

莺啼序·春晚感怀

吴文英

残寒正欺病酒，掩沉香绣户。燕来晚、飞入西城，似说春事迟暮。
画船载、清明过却，晴烟冉冉吴宫树。念羁情、游荡随风，
化为轻絮。

十载西湖，傍柳系马，趁娇尘软雾。溯红渐、招入仙溪，锦儿偷
寄幽素。倚银屏、春宽梦窄，断红湿、歌纨金缕。暝堤空，轻把
斜阳，总还鸥鹭。

幽兰旋老，杜若还生，水乡尚寄旅。别后访、六桥无信，事往花
委，瘗玉埋香，几番风雨。长波妒盼，遥山羞黛，渔灯分影春江
宿，记当时、短楫桃根渡。青楼仿佛。临分败壁题诗，
泪墨惨淡尘土。

危亭望极，草色天涯，叹鬓侵半苎。暗点检，离痕欢唾，尚染鲛
绡，亸凤迷归，破鸾慵舞。殷勤待写，书中长恨，蓝霞辽海沉过
雁，漫相思、弹入哀筝柱。伤心千里江南，怨曲重招，断魂在否？

Lines in Late Spring
To the Tune "Ying Ti Xu: Prologue of Orioles"
Wu Wenying

Remnant of late April cold: lashes my inebriated head: I shut
the window: light the agarwood: swallows
flit past the dim-lit city wall: from a single petal: they could tell
that spring is fading away: painted boats
float across the smoke-woven trees beside Wu Palace: already
another Qingming Festival: I lend my feelings
to the evening wind: my feelings visible as willow and poplar catkins:

A decade living beside West Lake: tying my horse to a tree:
a decade spent: stepping into the fragrant dust:
soft mist: tracing rows of red flowers that grow more red before
your chamber: a silk-bound letter that writes
to the end of love: love behind the silver paravent: dreams narrow
against the broad spring: vermilion tears smudged
the gold-laced robe: the embankment obscured, empty:
we pushed away the sun, returning it to gulls and herons:

Orchids grown old: pollia resurrected: I have secured my life
in this water town: I once returned to the Six Bridges:
time had retrieved your shadow: images of the past wilt: like flowers
in a cemetery of rain: your eyes envied by lake tides:

mountains rose to mimic the shape of your brows: a night on the river
in springtime: shadows lit by lamps on fish boats:
I recall now: the boat moved without oars: at the Peach Leaf dock:
the poem I wrote on the wall, mixed with ink
and tears: the words now illegible: dust rises: giving the wind its form:

At the high summerhouse: grass washes the earth:
light snow on my sideburns: I counted those old objects: the kerchief
tear-streaked: a look like the cut wings of a phoenix:
until air lifts it for an almost dance: there are more letters to be
written: long grief: but swan geese have drowned themselves
in the azure of the sky: nothing will reach you: I lend my pain
to a zither's strings: a song sweeping ten thousand acres
of Jiangnan: this melody to conjure your soul: will you not return: or
the world before me: already, appearances of your ghost:

虞美人·寄公度

舒亶

芙蓉落尽天涵水，日暮沧波起。
背飞双燕贴云寒，独向小楼东畔、倚阑看。

浮生只合尊前老，雪满长安道。
故人早晚上高台，赠我江南春色、一枝梅。

A Poem for Gong Du

To the Tune "Yu Mei Ren: The Beautiful Lady Yu"

Shu Dan

Friend, send me a stem
of plum blossoms by mail from Jiangnan.
By the time it arrives in my city,

the lotuses will be gone.
The waves will be tall in the autumn gusts.

Brief life—I permit myself growing old
before cups of wine. Suddenly,
snow filling every avenue in the capital.

念奴娇・春情

李清照

萧条庭院，又斜风细雨，重门须闭。
宠柳娇花寒食近，种种恼人天气。
险韵诗成，扶头酒醒，别是闲滋味。
征鸿过尽，万千心事难寄。

楼上几日春寒，帘垂四面，玉阑干慵倚。
被冷香消新梦觉，不许愁人不起。
清露晨流，新桐初引，多少游春意。
日高烟敛，更看今日晴未。

Feelings in Spring

To the Tune "Nian Nü Jiao: Remembering the Singing Lady"

Li Qingzhao

The courtyard seems more desolate in drizzle.
Doors must be latched.

Cold Food Festival is near with unpleasant weather.
I finished a new poem
with risky rhymes and a hangover.

To mail my feelings
those enlisted barn swallows are useless, as usual.

Spring chill is unbearable.
I put down curtains and don't even go on the balcony.
The coals burn out, so I must get up.

In dawn light and dew, the world seems floating.
Early sprouts of sycamore trees.

Should I take a walk
somewhere, like those happy, healthy people?

Let me wait for the sun to dissipate the mist then see
whether this is really a good day.

鹧鸪天·正月十一日观灯

姜夔

巷陌风光纵赏时。笼纱未出马先嘶。
白头居士无呵殿，只有乘肩小女随。

花满市，月侵衣。少年情事老来悲。
沙河塘上春寒浅，看了游人缓缓归。

Lantern Festival

To the Tune "Zhe Gu Tian: Partridge Sky"

Jiang Kui

The bustling streets teem with lanterns and tourists.
Horses neigh at the noble lady
who lifts her trailing furbelow to a palanquin.

I am a common citizen, making my shoulders
my daughter's palanquin.

The blossoms liquid-like, brimming
the bright marketplace. The moonlight infiltrates

my thin clothing with the chill of late spring.
This tour among the colorful lanterns

which once brought so much joy in my youthful years
carries a deep sorrow, finding me

at this old age. At Shahe Embankment,
tourists are holding hands, moving
slowly among the flowers, taking their time to leave.

戚氏·晚秋天

柳永

晚秋天，一霎微雨洒庭轩。槛菊萧疏，井梧零乱，惹残烟。
凄然，望江关，飞云黯淡夕阳间。
当时宋玉悲感，向此临水与登山。
远道迢递，行人凄楚，倦听陇水潺湲。
正蝉吟败叶，蛩响衰草，相应喧喧。

孤馆，度日如年。风露渐变，悄悄至更阑。
长天净，绛河清浅，皓月婵娟。
思绵绵。夜永对景，那堪屈指，暗想从前。
未名未禄，绮陌红楼，往往经岁迁延。

帝里风光好，当年少日，暮宴朝欢。
况有狂朋怪侣，遇当歌对酒竞留连。
别来迅景如梭，旧游似梦，烟水程何限。
念利名，憔悴长萦绊。追往事、空惨愁颜。漏箭移，稍觉轻寒。
渐呜咽，画角数声残。对闲窗畔，停灯向晓，抱影无眠。

Late Autumn
To the Tune "Qi Shi: The Surname Qi"

Liu Yong

Late autumn, the courtyard covered in a sheet of light rain.
The chrysanthemums toss their lean petals
beside the balustrade, and the leaves from a parasol tree,
unkempt on well water, stir the haze.

Desolate, I look out at the vast Yangtze:
the clouds aligned like fish scales rolling darkish
in twilight. Is this the same autumn
in Song Yu's grievous poetry against the cold cascade

and hills of destitution, mulling the death
of a world? The pathways infinite, where travelers, impoverished,
grow sick listening to the garrulous watercourses.
And the cicadas composing elegies for the dead leaves,

while the grasshoppers descant on their dying grass.
Their echoes grow more resounding as their end comes.
Alone at the post house, each hour
longer than a year. Toward midnight, autumn dew

grows infectious. My heart cold, my heart
like the long sky, clear with an unblemished moon,
but my thoughts come endless like mountain chains.
Curling my fingers, I recount my past,

my nameless and necessitous life, my body accepting
one lover after another
like a chair in a tavern. Too many years
wasted on dreaming and safekeeping the green sleeves

and crimson handkerchiefs stained
with lovers' copious tears. I think of my youthful years

living in the capital, drunk with so many friends
among inexhaustible scenes.

Banquets that lasted from dusk to morning and morning
to dusk, but then the departure—time
revolves like a spindle. Those streets of yesterday
like a trance, and the future unformed, vaporous,

as the morning fog on rivers
that dissolves the passing boats. This life enmeshed
in the web of fame and fortune
has only brought me a face distorted by sorrow.

The water clocks incessant as night turns frigid.
The distant bugle sounds like a sobbing horse.
I face the window; soon the lamplight will be replaced by dawn.
Long night, my shadow in my arms.

临江仙

李清照

庭院深深深几许？云窗雾阁常扃。
柳梢梅萼渐分明。春归秣陵树，人老建康城。

感月吟风多少事，如今老去无成。
谁怜憔悴更凋零。试灯无意思，踏雪没心情。

To the Tune "Lin Jiang Xian: Riverside Immortals"

Li Qingzhao

The courtyard deep in the deep shadow
of groves. The closed windows
further locked in by mist. Some trees
budding—the usual patterns of spring.
I think I'm going to die
in this region. My life spent singing
about the moon, the wind,
I accomplished nothing. I'm the only thing
withering away in Nanjing.
I have no desire to hang up the lanterns.
No desire to walk in the last snow.

Postscript

In the winter of 2022, a snowstorm blanketed Walla Walla, a Pacific Northwest city known for its sweet onions and wineries. I had taken a temporary teaching job there and rented a house with a backyard that opened onto woodlands, a pond, geese tracing patterns at dawn, and stags appearing at dusk. Through the patio door of my bedroom, the Blue Mountains stretched like a painting.

All night, the snow kept falling. As an immigrant who had spent nearly half my life in the States, writing in a second language far from home and family, I thought I understood solitude. But in this remote place—what Emily Dickinson might call "sumptuous Destitution"—I encountered a new depth of isolation. Otherworldly beauty existed alongside practical challenges; even Amazon deliveries struggled to reach us—that facial cream and soy sauce I ordered never arrived. I wanted to write. I stood on the balcony, searching for words to describe the snow. After a long silence, they came to me: 江国,正寂寂,叹寄与路遥,夜雪初积。

These weren't my words, but those of Jiang Kui, a poet from more than eight hundred years ago. He too was caught in a snowstorm at night, stranded in a world where travel depended on human feet, carriages, horses, and bamboo boats. Helplessly, he sighed over the absence of a beloved. I translated his lines into English: "The water provinces, desolate. // I want to send you this sprig of plum blossoms / tonight. Tonight, snow piles // for ten thousand miles."

In an age where the internet remembers for us, I didn't understand why Chinese education was so deeply rooted in memorization. My grandfather insisted I recite classical poetry before I could even read or write. He would read a line aloud, and I would echo it back, storing the rhymes and tone patterns by rote. In school, students spent hours each day, alone or in unison, committing ancient poems and rhymed prose to memory. By the time I left China, I had internalized hundreds.

But since adopting English, my internal anthology has eroded—poems dissolving into fragments, lines recombining like driftwood, forming a mental cento. Who would have thought that, one night in Walla Walla,

Jiang Kui's words would strike like lightning from centuries past, filling the dry creek of my speech?

The Language in Classical Chinese Poetry

It's challenging to translate ancient Chinese poetry. The language is inherently ambiguous. The language omits articles, linking verbs, and many conjunctions and prepositions, resulting in a syntax that lacks the clear, cause-and-effect structure of subject-verb-object. Additionally, nouns, verbs, and adjectives often interchange roles, and pronouns are rarely used; without explicit markers such as "I," "you," "it," or "we," the distinction between observer and observed becomes blurred, leaving emotions and images to float unanchored. The language relies heavily on juxtaposition and association. To illustrate this, consider a word-by-word reading of a poem by Du Fu—a glimpse into how a native Chinese reader might experience these ancient verses:

细	草	微	风	岸,	危	樯	独	夜	舟。
thin	grass	faint	wind	bank,	tall	mast	lone	night	boat

星	垂	平	野	阔,	月	涌	大	江	流。
star	hang	plain	wild	broad,	moon	gush	vast	river	flow

名	岂	文	章	著,	官	应	老	病	休。
fame	how	literary	essay	visible,	official	should	old	sick	end

飘	飘	何	所	似,	天	地	一	沙	鸥。
float	float	what	be	like,	sky	earth	one	sand	gull

In this version, characters function as independent checkpoints, along an invisible railway, that readers must connect imaginatively. The characters' isolated, open-ended meanings defy a straightforward translation into English. In ancient Chinese, every monosyllabic character forms a word with multiple potential meanings, with its specific sense crystallizing only when combined with others. They are malleable as toy bricks. Additionally, monosyllabic brevity often results in tightly fused adjective-noun or verb-noun compounds. I love the English word "sunset" for its dynamic quality—it melds the sun (noun) with its setting (verb) into a term that feels both active and static, like a moored boat undulating on water. It is more common in Chinese phrases to possess such duality.

In this poem, one might wonder about the relationship between juxtaposed phrases—such as "star hang" and "plain wild broad," or "moon gush" and "vast river flow." For instance, one English rendering of the couplet reads: "Stars hang low, making the plain wilderness seem broader. / The moonlight gushes along with the flow of a vast river." Immediately, we have a clearer sense of the situation—nouns find their definitive placement, fixed in relation to one another with the aid of modifiers—the adverb "low," the present participle "making," the definite article "the," the linking verb "seem," and the prepositional "along with" and "of." However, what's been compromised in this translation is the spatial interplay, the coexistence of events and elements, and multiple layers of meaning inherent in the source text. The line 月涌大江流, for example, exudes an almost surreal quality in Chinese—it conjures the image of the moon as a dam, which, once opened, unleashes an entire river.

The absence of prepositional phrases and linking verbs in Chinese poetry—as illustrated by the Du Fu poem—prevents actions and objects from being confined to fixed spatial coordinates or relationships. Similarly, the tenseless nature of classical Chinese poetry restrains it from committing to a finite segment of time. Because Chinese lacks verb tenses, there is no explicit differentiation among past, present, and future; shifts in time might be suggested through imagery—the transition of seasons, weather, historical events—or the narrative order—events presented in a specific sequence that the reader intuitively follows—or subtle textual cues such as stanza breaks or repetitions. Consider a poem by Li Shangyin:

君问归期未有期	You asked me a date of my return— no date has been set.
巴山夜雨涨秋池	Night rain falling on Ba Mountain swells the autumn ponds.
何当共剪西窗烛	When will we trim wicks together by our west window

却话巴山夜雨时 and talk about night rain falling on Ba Mountain?

It remains debatable whether Li Shangyin wrote the poem as a letter to his friend or as an elegy for his wife, who passed away a year before this poem was written. The first line—"You asked me a date of my return—no date has been set"—can be read as referring either to a past moment, when his wife was still alive, or to an imagined scenario. The second line grounds us in the present, as the poet observes the water level slowly rising in the ponds. The third line—"When will we trim wicks together by our west window"—recalls an intimate act that had happened in the past and may or may not repeat in the future, depending on whether the addressee is the friend or the dead wife. Finally, the closing line transports us to an imagined future, reflecting on "night rain falling on Ba Mountain," which is present. This interplay of past, present, and future creates a circular sense of timelessness—what one might call "all-timeness." The effect is made even more palpable in Chinese with the repetitions more pronounced, and the deliberate omission of linking verbs, prepositional phrases, and verb tenses that would confine events to a finite timeline. Instead, the poem returns to the inescapable phenomenon itself—the night rain on Ba Mountain, whose state of being undifferentiated, unpartitioned by the passage of time, seems to fall, is falling, and will continue to fall as it has fallen endlessly over a thousand years.

Allusions and Symbols in Chinese Poetry

"Poetry is the supreme result of the entire language," wrote Joseph Brodsky in "The Child of Civilization," elaborating that "poetry is, first of all, an art of references, allusions, linguistic and figurative parallels." This assertion is particularly evident in ancient poetry. Consider the Southern Song poet Xin Qiji's line 蛾眉曾有人妒—"moth brows were envied." In English, this phrase raises many questions. What are moth brows? Why were they envied, and by whom? Do moths even have brows? Even a more natural translation like "moth-like brows" feels peculiar. Why compare eyebrows to moths?

In classical Chinese, 蛾眉 (moth brows) refers to the shape of the waxing moon at the end of each lunar month. But why this comparison? The "moth" in the phrase refers to the silk moth, whose delicate antennae resemble the crescent moon. The phrase 蛾眉 first appeared in *Shijing*, China's oldest extant collection of poems from nearly three thousand years ago. One poem praises a woman's beauty: 螓首蛾眉—"with a forehead like a young cicada and brows like a silk moth." In a contemporary context, comparing a woman to insects might seem unflattering, even demeaning. But the ancient Chinese believed in a world without hierarchy—where all elements of nature were equally beautiful, worthy of meticulous observation. Over time, moth brows became a metonym for feminine beauty.

Seven centuries later, the poet Qu Yuan repurposed the phrase politically in "Li Sao": 众女疾余之蛾眉兮, 谣诼谓余以善淫—"the other women envy my moth brows, spreading rumors that I am lascivious and beguiling." For two thousand years, scholars interpreted "Li Sao" as an allegory of political persecution, a lament over Qu Yuan's exile. However, some have speculated that the poem expresses a homoerotic longing for King Huai of Chu. Either way, the phrase "moth brows" took on connotations of political defamation and banishment.

Thirteen hundred years after Qu Yuan drowned himself in the Miluo River, Xin Qiji revived 蛾眉, layering it with yet another political resonance. This time, it alluded to the banishment of Empress Chen in the Han dynasty, serving as a cipher for his own frustration—marginalized and exiled by the Southern Song court that favored appeasement over his call to reclaim lost territory.

Over three millennia, a single phrase—蛾眉—has thickened like porcelain, each poet adding a new layer of glaze. As Emerson remarked, "Language is fossil poetry. As the limestone of the continent consists of infinite masses of the shells of animalcules, so language is made up of images, or tropes, which now, in their secondary use, have long ceased to remind us of their poetic origin." Translating the "limestone"—the surface meaning of a poem—is simple. What is difficult is rendering the "infinite masses of the shells of animalcules"—the buried history behind each allusion.

Ancient Chinese poets lived in close communion with nature, filling their verses with blossoms, plants, and landscapes. Beyond their beauty, these natural elements carried symbolic resonance. Plum blossoms appear frequently throughout this book. The only flower to bloom in the dead of winter—a shock of scarlet against white snow—its blossoms became a symbol of purity, perseverance, and integrity, virtues the Song literati aspired to embody.

The plum blossom's literary roots trace back to *Shijing,* in the poem 摽有梅 ("Throwing the Plum Blossoms"), which expresses longing for marriage through the act of tossing plum blossoms to the ground. This association arises from a linguistic coincidence: 梅 (plum) is a homophone of 媒 (matchmaker or intermediary). Because of this, ancient Chinese poets saw the plum blossom as a living messenger, carrying a lover's heartbeat to the beloved. During the Northern and Southern dynasties, the poet Lu Kai deepened this association with longing when he wrote to a friend, 江南无所有, 聊赠一枝春—"All that is luminous in the spring of Jiangnan is this twig of plum blossoms, which I mail you." His simple gesture—offering a plum blossom as a token of remembrance—resonated with later poets, particularly those of the Song dynasty, who wove it into their own expressions of yearning and distance.

The plum blossom is but one illustration of a larger poetic tradition. In Chinese poetry, visual, homophonic, and literary associations are central. Another significant symbol in this book is the willow (柳, liǔ), which frequently appears in departure poems because its name sounds like "to stay" (留, liú), turning each willow tree into a silent plea for someone to remain. Similarly, silk (丝) is a homophone of "to miss someone" (思), imbuing the fabric with an air of longing. Geese, aside from evoking the legend of the Han diplomat Su Wu, form shapes in the autumn sky that suggest the characters 一 (one, symbolizing unity) and 人 (people, symbolizing humanity), therefore becoming a common messenger in these poems. Additionally, "cardamom" serves as a metonym for a young girl around twelve or thirteen years old, eventually symbolizing youth. The moon carries more than a hundred metonymic meanings and monikers in Chinese literature, while in English it has one name: "the moon."

A Brief History of Ci

It is believed that earliest ci originated in Sui dynasty (581–618). The reunification of China proper during the short-lived Sui laid the foundation for the Tang dynasty (618–907) to prosper economically through trade along both the Silk Road and maritime routes. While porcelain, tea, silk brocade, and lacquerware were exported as far as Egypt, Rome, and Greece, foreign products and cultural influences also flushed into China—dates, spinach, and pistachio nuts from Persia; spices from India; and honey, camels, and wine from Central Asia. Alongside these lucrative commodities came dances and music.

The origin of ci remains obscure. Largely developed in the late Tang, ci is believed to have drawn on the traditions of 乐府 (folk song–style bureau music) as well as the melodies and performance customs of Central Asia. As trade expanded, markets, festivals, taverns, restaurants, and singing houses flourished, giving rise to a vibrant entertainment industry. Early ci, mostly anonymous, are thought to have been composed by music performers, song girls, and prostitutes, reflecting the vernacular of the common people. The earliest 曲子词 (song lyrics), found in the ancient trading center and garrison town Dunhuang, stand out for their bold, frivolous, and explicit language, with themes predominantly centered on love and the sorrow stirred by separation. Unsurprisingly, most patrons at the northwest border of China were Silk Road travelers: businessmen, soldiers, and nomads, for whom the feelings of separation, nostalgia, and longing for loved ones resonated. It wasn't long before ci gained widespread popularity among the elite, transitioning from taverns, street markets, and singing houses to the imperial court and private gatherings of literati and government officials.

During the Song dynasty (960–1279), the form of ci reached its peak. This was an era marked by social stability, technological innovation, and economic prosperity. Notably, paper money was first issued, the compass and gunpowder weapons were invented, medicine and forensic science were developed, and new crops were introduced, causing the population to double in size between the tenth and eleventh centuries. Private academies, temples, public clinics, retirement homes, and various social clubs flourished, while movable printing technology facilitated the widespread dissemination of literature, history, religion, and philosophy. Most importantly, reforms to the imperial examinations ushered in meritocracy and social mobility, transitioning the empire's administration from aristocratic families to nonaristocratic civil servants. The literati of the time, trained in neo-Confucian philosophy and classical poetry for the examinations, also cultivated their skills in landscape painting, calligraphy, go, and music. In fact, many scholar-officials were poets—so much so that the era was sometimes described as one in which the empire was run by poets—including high-ranking officials such as Yan Shu, Wang Anshi, Fan Zhongyan, Ouyang Xiu, and Su Shi.

Among Song poets, there was a growing sense that Tang poets had already perfected and exhausted the revered shi form. As a result, when ci—rooted in oral, colloquial tradition—emerged, it quickly became a favorite. As the educated literati adopted the form, they embraced an aesthetic of subtlety and indirectness, though their enduring preoccupation with the theme of romance remained. Many early ci poems celebrate reunion, mourn separation, and urge indulgence in fleeting pleasures—a poetic carpe diem. This awareness of transience also gave rise to another central motif in Song ci: 伤春悲秋 (spring melancholy and autumn grief), a sentiment that seems to echo across poets throughout cultures and history.

The Chinese adage 诗言志, 词缘情—"shi expresses aspiration, while ci conveys emotion"—captures, albeit imperfectly, the thematic weight of ci poetry. In early Northern Song, ci primarily served as banquet entertainment, performed by hired women yet composed almost exclusively by men. This created a peculiar dynamic where men wrote lyrics about desire in the voices of women to be sung back to them by women. Perhaps even more twisted, many of these love poems doubled as veiled expressions of political frustration. A woman's wait for her beloved could be read as a metaphor for an official's longing for recognition from the court and emperor.

"That's what I love about ci," a young Chinese scholar told me when I returned to Chengdu, often called the gay capital of China. He explained that since ci is typically performed by singing courtesans, poets had to craft lyrics whose intonations and tunes suited the female voice—ci was a form of ventriloquism. Yet skilled poets often inadvertently infused their work with their own knowledge, aspirations, and personal refinement. As a result, ci often possesses a distinctly androgynous and queer quality. Especially in its early stages, the male speaker, longing for his beloved, had to step outside his masculine identity, adopting the persona of his female partner to address himself—"I" pretend to be "you" so "I" can speak to "me"; the "I" must first be abandoned to speak and be heard.

By the eleventh century, ci had been expanded and refined by a growing group of poets, most notably Liu Yong and Su Shi—two figures who could not have been more different. Liu Yong, an ambitious young man who aspired to a political career, failed the imperial examinations four times; he spent much of his life in singing houses and brothels, writing ci in exchange for lodging, wine, and meals—making him the first professional ci poet. Su Shi, by contrast, attained the highest jinshi degree in the imperial examinations at just nineteen and went on to have a distinguished career in government, holding high-ranking positions both at the provincial and central court.

Liu Yong developed the form of 慢词 (long song, or slow tune), which featured longer lines, fewer rhymes, and a measured, prose-like rhythm. His time in brothels also influenced his work, as he incorporated colloquial and even vulgar speech, making the male speakers in his poems strikingly genuine, vulnerable, and frail—a style that drew heavy criticism from his contemporaries. By expanding the length and structure of ci, Liu paved the way for later poets such as Zhou Bangyan, Jiang Kui, and Wu Wenying to experiment with extended scene-setting, the passage of time, circular structures, emotional counterpoints, and nonlinear narratives.

Su Shi expanded the thematic and stylistic range of ci, incorporating diction, subject matter, and techniques that had previously been reserved for shi poetry. One of the most accomplished figures in Chinese history, he excelled in nearly every field—calligraphy, painting, politics, engineering, architecture, gastronomy, and travel writing. He was also one of the greatest essayists of his time. Despite his success, Su's career was marked by political exile, during which his poetry flourished. He wrote about nearly everything in his daily life—conversations with peasants and woodsmen, ekphrasis, biting sarcasm aimed at his political opponents, social commentary, historical reflection, and even the pleasures of crab meat and pomegranates. In the Southern Song dynasty, Xin Qiji carried Su's legacy forward. By the end of both Liu's and Su's lives, ci was no longer merely popular songs. Though it continued to be sung and circulated in social gatherings, it had evolved into a serious literary art form.

The Form of Ci

The poetic form ci (词), meaning "lyrics," emerged during the Tang dynasty as shi (诗) poetry reached its peak. Initially considered inferior to shi, ci was often dismissed as 诗馀—literally, "poetry's remnants" or "poetry besides shi." Shi, meaning "poetry," consists of two etymological components: "word" (言) and "temple" (寺), reflecting its deep cultural and ritual significance. Shi traces its origins to the *Shijing* (*Classic of Poetry*), an anthology of 305 poems dating from the eleventh to seventh centuries BCE, traditionally attributed to Confucius as its editor and compiler. Over time, the *Shijing* became a cornerstone of Confucian thought and a foundational text for the imperial examination system.

The most distinctive formal characteristic of Tang dynasty shi is its fixed structure, typically composed of four or eight lines, with each line containing a set number of characters, usually five or seven. In regulated verse forms such as lüshi and jueju, strict rules govern verbal and tonal parallelism—lines are arranged in couplets where the second line mirrors the first in syntax, meaning, imagery, and tone. By contrast, the defining features of ci are its irregular line length and more flexible rhyme placement. This variability gives ci its alternate name: 长短句 (long-and-short sentences). To illustrate these structural and rhythmic differences, let's compare a shi poem from the Tang dynasty with a ci poem from the Song dynasty:

鹿柴

空山不见人，	kōng shān bú jiàn rén
但闻人语响。	dàn wén rén yǔ **xiǎng**
返景入深林，	fǎn jǐng rù shēn lín
复照青苔上。	fù zhào qīng tái **shàng**

Luzhai

Wang Wei

An empty mountain, no one in sight.
But I hear echoes of human words.
A sash of light enters the deep forest,
glimmering on the dark green moss.

This well-known shi poem by Wang Wei exemplifies the highly structured form of Tang poetry. It follows the wuyan jueju (五言绝句) form, a five-character-per-line symmetrical quatrain with a volta in between the second and third lines. The poem has an almost square-like visual balance. Each syllable's tonal pattern is fixed, much like the meter in English poetry. Every line is end-stopped, following a rhythmic structure known as judou (句读). The motion in Chinese is typically read as 1-2 / 3-4-5, creating a steady and measured cadence. Compare this to a long-song ci by Liu Yong:

雨霖铃

寒蝉凄切, 对长亭晚, 骤雨初歇。	hán chán qī **qiè**, duì cháng tíng wǎn, zhòu yǔ chū **xiē**
都门帐饮无绪, 留恋处, 兰舟催发。	dū mén zhàng yǐn wú xù, liú liàn chù, lán zhōu cuī fā
执手相看泪眼, 竟无语凝噎。	zhí shǒu xiāng kàn lèi yǎn, jìng wú yǔ níng **yē**
念去去, 千里烟波, 暮霭沉沉楚天阔。	niàn qù qù, qiān lǐ yān **bō**, mù ǎi chén chén chǔ tiān **kuò**
多情自古伤离别, 更那堪, 冷落清秋节!	duō qíng zì gǔ shāng lí **bié**, gèng nǎ kān, lěng luò qīng qiū **jié**
今宵酒醒何处? 杨柳岸, 晓风残月。	jīn xiāo jiǔ xǐng hé chù? Yang liu àn, xiǎo fēng cán **yuè**
此去经年, 应是良辰好景虚设。	cǐ qù jīng nián, yīng shì liáng chén hǎo jǐng xū shè
便纵有千种风情, 更与何人说?	biàn zòng yǒu qiān zhǒng fēng qíng, gèng yǔ hé rén **shuō**?

To the Tune "Yu Lin Ling: Bells in Rain"

Liu Yong

The sound of cicadas pierces

the autumn sky; late against the pavilion,
the downpour stops

so suddenly. At the makeshift tent,
beyond the city gate of the capital, the wine,

tasteless. The docked boat
like a leaf of magnolia urges your leaving.

We hold hands, looking
so deeply into each other's eyes, tearful—

for the first time, I feel that more language
suggests more hopelessness.

Thinking of where
you are going—you are going

where masses of evening clouds envelop,
thicken over an infinite

stretch of mist-hooded waters.

Those who laugh at me
for my sentimentality, come, step inside

this lover's shape
that cuts open this desolate autumn day.

To what will I wake
tonight? At the bank of poplars and willows,

where the dawn wind shears a slim moon.
There will still be years

ahead, good days that are embroideries
with enchanting images

continuing in emptiness. How they will invoke
a thousand feelings—a thousand

ravishments, agonies—
and I can't tell you about any of it.

The title of a ci poem—such as "Yu Lin Ling: Bells in Rain"—often has no direct connection to the poem's subject. Instead, it indicates the tune or formal pattern to which the poem was composed, as ci were originally written to be sung. These tune names often carry historical or literary allusions, though we won't elaborate here. The system is somewhat analogous to technical titles in classical music—such as Violin Concerto in D Major or Minuet in G Minor—where the structure precedes the content.

In ci, the lines flow with a more elastic and unpredictable rhythm, reinforced by shifting rhymes. It's important to note that ancient Chinese literature lacked punctuation and line breaks, meaning that rhythmic pauses were entirely guided by caesuras. For example, the first line of "Yu Lin Ling" should be read hán chán / qī qiè, / duì / cháng tíng wǎn, / zhòu yǔ / chū xiē, a tempo I tried to somehow echo in English translation with line breaks, stresses, and enjambment, "The sound of cicadas pierces / the autumn sky; / late against the pavilion, / the downpour stops." The fluidity and irregular movement within ci not only made it an ideal vessel for expressing protracted and complex emotions but also aligned it with musical phrasing when performed.

While ci appears to allow more formal freedom than shi, the truth is, it operates under a more rigid structure. The irregular line lengths are not arbitrary; they adhere to an unyielding matrix of syllable counts, rhyme schemes, tempo, and tonal patterns, all of which have to match specific musical scales. The process was so meticulous and even mechanical that in the Song dynasty, one did not speak of "writing" ci, but of 填词 or "filling in" ci, fitting lyrics to an existing melody or structural framework.

So, there's this irony: The complete subjugation of language created an illusion of freedom in the language.

My Translation

Because of the unique linguistic and structural features in Chinese, English translations in this book often triple or quadruple the original Chinese length. While the gap between Song ci and modern Chinese is not as vast as that between *Beowulf* and modern English, it is substantial enough that translation can sometimes feel like explanation. For example, Xin Qiji was one of my favorite Song poets until I started translating his work; the English version can be twenty times longer than the original. In a twelve-sentence poem, "Sending Off My Cousin Mao Jia," he used seven literary and historical allusions and stories, which are equivalent to a whole short story collection. Consider the literal translation of two lines from the poem:

> 马上琵琶关塞黑，更长门、翠辇辞金阙。看燕燕，送归妾。
> 将军百战身名裂。向河梁、回头万里，故人长绝。

> On horseback, [ ] pipa—borderland darkens,
> let alone at Long Gate, [ ] jade palanquin takes leave
> of the gold palace. Swallows send back wife.
>
> General, after a hundred battles, ruins his fame.
> On the riverbank, [ ] turns back:
> ten thousand miles—farewell to an old friend.

The brackets refer to the missing subjects in the sentence. This rendering raises immediate questions about the subject of each action and the connectivity of events: Who is on the horseback holding a pipa? What transpires at the borderland? What happens at Long Gate that instigates this departure of a jade palanquin? Who's on it? Who is the wife? Which general turns back, and for whom? Each question hints at a rich tapestry of historical events and literary allusions that Chinese readers can grasp intuitively. To avoid using notes at the back of the book, like an ingredient list on the back of canned food, I decided to retell these stories within the span of the poem, translating a lyric poem into a narrative one.

The Southern Song poet Wu Wenying is notoriously difficult to read, let alone to translate. He was an avant-garde force in his time, using highly ornate, fragmentary language and constantly shifting moods and temporal settings within a single line. His poems wind like a vertiginous labyrinth, filled with invented metonyms that make the familiar strange. Some have even described his work as "watching the blossoms across a river of mist."

The first poem I translated from Wu begins with the line 润玉笼绡, 檀樱倚扇, which literally reads, "Warm and moist jade covered in silk gauze; a sandalwood-scented, crimson cherry leans on a folding fan." But there's a subtext: "jade" stands for a wrist or arm, "silk gauze" evokes sleeves, and the word 檀 carries the dual meanings of sandal scent and crimson hue, while "cherry" suggests lips. In effect, the line portrays the beloved's wrist enveloped in sleeves and her lips partly hidden behind a folding fan.

Wu's poems work on the metonymic level, though metonyms work best when they are part of a shared cultural code. However, Wu intentionally defamiliarizes this cultural code by using elliptical diction and inventing his own metonyms. The line is not a metaphor either; it doesn't have the words "arm," "sleeve," or "lip" in it. If the metaphor works as "A is B," then Wu removes the A completely and presents only B, demanding the reader to infer the presence of A through the context of the poem. So, it would be an injustice to translate it as a metaphor or simile—"her wrist is like jade" and "her lips are like cherries." I decided to take a risk by presenting both the literal and figurative simultaneously in English as parallels, using colons as bonds. I also wanted to preserve Wu's embellished Chinese by stylizing the English translation: "The jade's sleek skin leaks scrubbed light: / arm bare, chiffon / swathed: a quarter slice of cherry / shaken by its own reddening: lips / concealed behind a folding fan's / unfolding."

While I was finishing this book, many Chinese friends, ardent fans of ci, asked if I had translated their favorites (all Chinese grew up reciting them). Almost always, I had to say no. There are some of my personal favorites that I found too challenging to translate. Take Li Qingzhao's famous opening, 寻寻觅觅, 冷冷清清, 凄凄惨惨戚戚; translating that feels like witnessing Gerard Manley Hopkins's "Spelt from Sibyl's Leaves" being butchered in Chinese—I couldn't bring myself to do it. Similarly, Xin Qiji's renowned line 众里寻他千百度。蓦然回首, 那人却在, 灯火阑珊处 resisted any English expression that could capture its precise sentiment. I tried to translate and failed. I chose to leave these poems untranslated, convinced that some poems are too enmeshed in the music of their language—music becomes the very meaning of the poem—to be fully recreated in another tongue.

My literary world was shaped by translations: Growing up, I stole books from my father's library, devouring Byron, Pushkin, Goethe, Rilke, Tagore, Baudelaire, Neruda, Chateaubriand—and by middle school, with my allowance I started buying Chinese translations of Lorca, Mann, Tsvetaeva, Proust, Trakl, Aygi, and more. I learned this language of English in order to hear Shakespeare sing. Recently, when a friend asked who best translates Cavafy, I couldn't choose—Rae Dalven's and Edmund Keeley and Philip Sherrard's versions each feel indispensable, much like asking who plays Beethoven's sonatas best: Backhaus, Schnabel, or Gilels? Each brings subtle nuances and distinctive interpretations. To miss one album is to miss a whole world. To me, translators are like musicians, interpreting and unfolding distant worlds for their audience.

In the movie *Nostalghia,* Oleg Yankovsky declares, "Poetry is untranslatable, like the whole of art." In translation, the original is shattered and its fragments reassembled into a different entity—an exile that neither fully embodies the source's beauty nor feels completely at home in its new linguistic habitat. These translations drift like space debris between the native and the foreign. There's a detachment in such floating movement and a freedom in such aimlessness. Consequently, by their malleable nature, translations are always in flux, ready to be reshaped, rearranged, and reinvented. Nothing resides in the definite.

Perhaps this is the ideal poetry—restlessly seeking a perfect form, tone, lexicon, and texture, without ever conciliating with a singular identity. The poems never seem to be comfortable enough on the page, being chained in strange syllables and rhythms they are not born with. Such deliberate unease, I hope, will be perceptible to the readers. A knowledgeable reader might find agreement and dissent simultaneously in the same poem—the translation, a bridge that connects and disconnects the shores of two languages, that estranges the landscapes of both languages. Language is the structure through which we experience and interpret the world. By shattering this structure, even with a small crevice, I hope that with that slim infiltrating light, we can view the rigid world a little differently than before.

Acknowledgments

I have benefited from friends' patient eyes, keen ears, and insightful scholarship that helped shape this book. I am thankful to Forrest Gander, Yuki Tanaka, Huang Shun, Johann Sarna, Robert Dale Parker, Tang Xiaolong, Robert Hass, C. Francis Fisher, E Tu, and Arthur Sze for their invaluable guidance and encouragement. I owe a special debt to Daniel Ruiz, Yunqin Wang, Ruoyun Chen, and Jane Miller, who generously and tirelessly read countless iterations of this manuscript; your rigorous, passionate feedback became indelible echoes in these translations. To the interminable snow in Walla Walla, the riotous blossoms in California, and the ocean in Boston. In loving memory of Dean Young and Louise Glück. I am indebted to my editor, Michael Wiegers, whose generosity and trust made this book possible, and to the outstanding team at Copper Canyon Press. I am grateful to the editors of the following journals, where early versions of these translations first appeared: *The Adroit Journal, Alaska Quarterly Review, The Common, Denver Quarterly, Emergence Magazine, Oxford Poetry, Peripheries, Poetry,* and *The Yale Review.* I also wish to thank Whitman College, the Mass Cultural Council, and my colleagues and students at the University of Massachusetts Boston for granting me the precious time and support to complete this work. To my grandfather Fang Qingyang, who passed down volumes of threadbare books of the original Chinese poems and taught me to memorize, sing them before I could even read—thank you for planting their music deep within me.

Biographies of Poets

无名氏 ANONYMOUS is a figure who could be anyone, perhaps the greatest poet spanning cultures and histories.

陈与义 CHEN YUYI (1090–1138) was a poet-politician during the transitional period between the Northern and Southern Song. An official in the central government, he excelled in shi poetry, contributing some of the finest works of the Song era, but only dabbled in the ci poetry form.

范仲淹 FAN ZHONGYAN (989–1052), a military strategist, philosopher, poet, and politician of the Northern Song dynasty, held various regional posts, including magistrate for the Jiqing Army and salt-store inspector. Known for his dike-building projects along the coast and for educational advances, he initiated the Qingli Reforms that later inspired Chancellor Wang Anshi. As prime minister of the entire Song empire, he left a lasting literary legacy through philosophical and political essays that advocated for his precept "Better remonstrate and die, than keep silent and live." He is also known for his shi poetry, with only five ci poems remaining.

贺铸 HE ZHU (1052–1125), a military officer turned civil servant, retired to Suzhou toward the end of the Northern Song. Renowned for both prose and poetry, he earned the nickname Ghost Head He due to his reputed ugliness. Famous for his poetic line about plums, "If you ask me to describe my sorrow—that sudden rain when plums turn yellow," he is also known as Plum He.

蒋捷 JIANG JIE (1245–1305) was celebrated for the lightness of his language, his intricate musicality, and the invention of nuanced poetic phrases. In 1274, he achieved the jinshi degree, the highest honor in the imperial examination. Following the fall of the Southern Song, Jiang Jie refused to serve the Yuan court and vanished from public life. Renowned for his evocative line "The floating light of days, leaving us behind, reddens the cherries, greens the plantains," he earned the title Jinshi of the Red Cherry.

姜夔 Jiang Kui (1155–1221), a poet, composer, musicologist, and calligrapher of the Southern Song dynasty, gained prominence as one of the most influential ci poets. Unlike many contemporaries, he abstained from a government career. He lived an impoverished life, sustaining himself by selling his calligraphic works.

李重元 Li Chongyuan (circa 1122) is known for his four surviving poems, each with a title including a season: spring, summer, autumn, and winter.

李清照 Li Qingzhao (1084–1155), poet and essayist of the Song dynasty, hailed from a prestigious scholar-official family. Married to the poet-politician Zhao Mingcheng, she collected with her husband numerous books, sculptures in bronze and stone, paintings, and calligraphies, lost during the Jin-Song Wars. The couple often wrote love poems as letters to each other, even as playful competition, when Zhao was absent from home for official work. Of course, Li always won. Zhao died of typhoid fever on the route to an official post during the Jin-Song Wars. Li never recovered. Her later life was marked by imprisonment, exile, and poverty. She kept working to complete her postscript to the *Jinshilu* (Catalogue of inscriptions on metal and stone), a book that mentioned the documents she and Zhao had collected and viewed. She wrote poetry till the end of her life and is regarded as one of the greatest poets in Chinese history.

刘辰翁 Liu Chenweng (1232–1297) was a poet and literary critic at the end of the Southern Song dynasty. Following the Mongolian army's occupation, he embraced a hermit's life, dedicating himself to writing.

刘过 Liu Guo (1154–1206) lived and wrote during the Southern Song dynasty.

柳永 Liu Yong (984–1053) is credited with inventing the manci (long song). After failing four times the imperial examination, he wrote, "I'm willing to trade this empty pursuit of political fame for lifelong drinking and soft songs." For this poem, the emperor banished him from future government employment and asked him to write lyrics for the rest of his life. He described his career sarcastically as "writing poems under the heavenly command of the emperor." His ci poems brought him peerless fame across the nation, but the literati high society of the time wrote essays assailing his work as vulgar kitsch for its despicable subjects and colloquial manners. He died impoverished and unable to afford his own coffin, and the song girls to whom he dedicated most of his poems raised funds for his burial.

吕本中 Lü Benzhong (1084–1145) was a poet, politician, and Taoist of the Northern Song dynasty.

陆游 Lu You (1125–1210), born at the end of the Northern Song dynasty, dedicated his life to advocating for a northern expedition to reclaim lost land. Removed from office for his patriotic stance, he penned a poignant shi poem at the end of his life: "The night deepens, a storm beyond my window. / The ironclad horses and the ice river invade my dream."

欧阳修 Ouyang Xiu (1007–1072), a prominent historian, calligrapher, epigrapher, essayist, poet, and politician during the Northern Song dynasty, played a key role in reviving the Classical Prose Movement. Holding several influential positions in the early 1060s, including assistant chief councillor, Hanlin academician, vice commissioner of military affairs, and vice minister of revenues, he earned renown for his prose and historical works. Referring to himself as Zui Weng, or Drunken Old Man, he was also the teacher of Su Shi. He dedicated his literary practice to essays and shi poems, and showed limited interest in ci poems.

秦观 Qin Guan (1049–1100) was a politician and poet during the Northern Song dynasty. He studied under Su Shi. In 1083, his rhymed-prose fu earned him the position of chief of learning in the National Academy. Renowned for his contributions to ci poetry, he was admired for ornate diction, allusive expression, and a sophisticated musical sense. His famous line about clouds above a mountain led to his moniker Scholar of the Mountain Dappled by Thin Clouds.

舒亶 SHU DAN (1042–1104) was a poet and politician of the Northern Song dynasty. His poetry is noted for its elegance, concision, and inventive depth. As a politician, Shu Dan played a controversial role in prosecuting Wang Anshi and Su Shi. He was instrumental in the infamous Crow Terrace Poetry Trial, where Su Shi faced charges of treason and lese majesty, with Su Shi's poetry presented as evidence against him. This trial became a pivotal moment in the history of free speech in medieval China, ultimately leading to Su Shi's conviction and exile.

苏轼 SU SHI (1037–1101), also known as Su Dongpo, was a multifaceted figure in the Northern Song dynasty. He excelled in poetry, essays, calligraphy, painting, gastronomy, and travel writing. He had a lengthy career in bureaucracy, including briefly serving as a senior official at the imperial court. Su Shi faced political challenges due to his outspoken criticism and involvement in rivalries, and his creative career flourished during periods of political exile. He is one of the most accomplished figures in classical Chinese literature. Among his many contributions is the famous dish Dongpo meat, a preparation of pork belly that is pan-fried and then red-cooked, a beloved culinary classic in China.

王安石 WANG ANSHI (1021–1086) was an economist, philosopher, poet, and politician during the Northern Song dynasty. He served as chancellor and attempted major and controversial socioeconomic reforms known collectively as the New Policies. He was one of the earliest writers of ci, but he wrote very little and focused primarily on prose.

吴文英 WU WENYING (1205–1260), a poet in the Southern Song dynasty, is often regarded as the avant-garde of ci poets. His poems are celebrated for dense imagery, idiosyncratic euphemisms, nonlinearity, and dream logic, earning him the moniker Li Shangyin of Ci Poets.

辛弃疾 XIN QIJI (1140–1207) was a poet, calligrapher, and military general during the Southern Song dynasty. His grandfather named him after a legendary military commander from the Western Han, hoping he would recover the occupied land of the Northern Song. At the age of twenty-two, he commanded fifty cavalries and fought through thousands of soldiers. This victory gained Xin a place in the Southern Song court, which supported an appeasement policy. His advocacy was silenced, and he was sidelined to remote provinces, where he improved irrigation systems and helped relocate peasants—and wrote poems for forty years. Xin's poems achieved a balance between direct and bold tones and dense, sophisticated literary and historical allusions.

晏几道 YAN JIDAO (1038–1110), the youngest son of statesman and poet Yan Shu, was born into an aristocratic household. But his life was marked by dramatic misfortune; he was seventeen when his influential father passed away. Despite his gifts and connections, he chose a life of poverty, refusing to use his talents to advance socially. Yan is celebrated as a master of romance-themed short songs, which often evoke memories of lost love and fleeting pleasures. The motif of the dream appears frequently throughout his works. He gave himself the art name Little Mountain.

晏殊 YAN SHU (991–1055), a renowned poet, politician, calligrapher, and essayist of the Northern Song dynasty, displayed extraordinary talent from a young age. By seven, he was already recognized for his poetry and essays, and at fourteen, he earned the jinshi degree, the highest honor in the imperial examination. Over a long official career, he held various central and regional posts under two emperors and served as prime minister. A prolific writer of ci poetry, Yan Shu is said to have composed over 10,000 ci, though only about 136 survive. His fame in ci poetry was later overshadowed by that of his son, Yan Jidao.

俞国宝 YU GUOBAO (circa 1195) was a poet of the Southern Song dynasty. He was known for one of his poems being praised—and having one phrase revised—by Emperor Gaozong of Song.

张先 ZHANG XIAN (990–1078), a poet and politician of the Northern Song dynasty, earned the epithet Zhang of Three Shadows for his notable use of the word *shadow*.

张孝祥 ZHANG XIAOXIANG (1132–1170) was a poet and politician of the Southern Song dynasty. In an era marked by conflict, he exhibited a strong sense of patriotism, as reflected in his ci, which are celebrated for their audacious artistic expression. Dissatisfied with the political climate of the Southern Song court, he chose to resign from his position. He passed away at the age of thirty-eight.

张镃 Zhang Zi (1153–circa 1235), a literatus and government official from a distinguished military family, became entangled in a political coup while serving in the agricultural sector. His life ended following the plot's failure and his subsequent removal from the court.

赵佶 Zhao Ji (1082–1135), also known as Huizong of Song, was the eighth emperor of the Song dynasty and the penultimate emperor of the Northern Song. Widely regarded as one of China's greatest painters and calligraphers, he invented the influential Slender Gold style of calligraphy, which mimics the twists and turns of gold filaments. Huizong indulged in luxury, sophistication, and art, with interests in architecture, garden design, and even medicine and Taoism. But his extravagant pursuits led to disastrous consequences for the nation. In 1126, when the Jurchen-led Jin dynasty invaded the Song, the capital, Bianjing, was conquered. Huizong and his family were taken captive by the Jurchens and brought to the Jin capital, an event known as the Shame of Jingkang. Emperor Taizong of Jin gave Huizong the humiliating title of Duke Hunde (Besotted Duke). Huizong is often included in lists of both the greatest artists of ancient China and the worst emperors of ancient China. His poem included here was written during his captivity in the Jin capital.

赵令畤 Zhao Lingzhi (1064–1134) was a poet and politician of the Northern Song dynasty.

周邦彦 Zhou Bangyan (1056–1121), a musician, poet, and politician of the Northern Song dynasty, held the position of director of the palace library. Revered for his expertise in metrical forms and music, he was known as the Crown of Ci Poets and the Du Fu of Ci Poets.

About the Translator

方商羊 Shangyang Fang grew up in Chengdu, China. He is the author of *Burying the Mountain.*

POETS FOR POETRY

Copper Canyon Press poets are at the center of all our efforts as a nonprofit publisher. Poets create the art of our books, and they read and teach the books we publish. Many are also generous donors who believe in financially supporting the vibrant poetry community of Copper Canyon Press. For decades, our poets have quietly donated their royalties, have contributed their time to our fundraising campaigns, and have made personal donations in support of emerging and established poets. Their generosity has encouraged the innovative risk-taking that sustains and furthers the art form.

The donor-poets who have contributed to the Press since 2023 include:

Jonathan Aaron
Pamela Alexander
Kazim Ali
Ellen Bass
Erin Belieu
Mark Bibbins
Linda Bierds
Sherwin Bitsui
Jaswinder Bolina
Marianne Boruch
Laure-Anne Bosselaar
Cyrus Cassells
Peter Cole and Adina Hoffman
Elizabeth J. Coleman
Shangyang Fang
John Freeman
Forrest Gander
Jenny George
Dan Gerber
Jorie Graham
Roger Greenwald
Robert and Carolyn Hedin
Bob Hicok
Ha Jin
The estate of Jaan Kaplinski
Laura Kasischke
Jennifer L. Knox
Ted Kooser
Stephen Kuusisto
Deborah Landau
Sung-Il Lee
Ben Lerner
Dana Levin
Maurice Manning
Heather McHugh
Jane Miller
Roger Mitchell
Lisa Olstein
Gregory Orr
Eric Pankey
Kevin Prufer
Alicia Rabins
Dean Rader
Paisley Rekdal
James Richardson
Alberto Ríos
David Romtvedt
Sarah Ruhl
Kelli Russell Agodon
Natalie Shapero
Arthur Sze
Yuki Tanaka
Elaine Terranova
Chase Twichell
Ocean Vuong
Connie Wanek
Emily Warn

Poetry is vital to language and living. Since 1972, Copper Canyon Press has published extraordinary poetry from around the world to engage the imaginations and intellects of readers, writers, booksellers, librarians, teachers, students, and donors.

WE ARE GRATEFUL FOR THE MAJOR SUPPORT PROVIDED BY:

academy of american poets

TO LEARN MORE ABOUT UNDERWRITING COPPER CANYON PRESS TITLES, PLEASE CALL 360-385-4925 EXT. 105

We are grateful for the major support provided by:

Anonymous
Jill Baker and Jeffrey Bishop
Anne and Geoffrey Barker
Mona Baroudi and Patrick Whitgrove
Lisha Bian
Rick Shinsui Bowles
John Branch
Diana Broze
John R. Cahill
Sarah J. Cavanaugh
Keith Cowan and Linda Walsh
Peter Currie
Geralyn White Dreyfous
The Evans Family
Mimi Gardner Gates
Claire Gribbin
Gull Industries Inc. on behalf of William True
Carolyn and Robert Hedin
David and Jane Hibbard
Bruce S. Kahn
Phil Kovacevich and Eric Wechsler
Eric La Brecque
Maureen Lee and Mark Busto
Ellie Mathews and Carl Youngmann as The North Press
Kathryn O'Driscoll
Petunia Charitable Fund and advisor Elizabeth Hebert
Suzanne Rapp and Mark Hamilton
Adam and Lynn Rauch
Emily and Dan Raymond
Joseph C. Roberts
Cynthia Sears
Kim and Jeff Seely
Tree Swenson
Julia Sze
Donna Wolf
Jamie Wolf
Barbara and Charles Wright
In honor of C.D. Wright from Forrest Gander
Caleb Young as C. Young Creative
The dedicated interns and faithful volunteers of Copper Canyon Press

The pressmark for Copper Canyon Press
suggests entrance, connection, and interaction
while holding at its center
an attentive, dynamic space for poetry.

This book is set in Adobe Garamond Pro.
Book design by Gopa & Ted2, Inc.
Printed on archival-quality paper.